Thinking

Games for

KiDS

UPDATED EDITION

Cheryl Gerson Tuttle

Penny Hutchins Paquette

McGraw·Hill

New York   Chicago   San Francisco   Lisbon   London   Madrid   Mexico City
Milan   New Delhi   San Juan   Seoul   Singapore   Sydney   Toronto

The *McGraw·Hill* Companies

Library of Congress Cataloging-in-Publication Data

Tuttle, Cheryl Gerson.
    Thinking games for kids / Cheryl Gerson Tuttle, Penny Hutchins Paquette. —
updated ed.
        p.   cm.
    New ed. of : Thinking games to play with your child : easy ways to develop creative and
critical thinking skills / Cheryl Gerson Tuttle, Penny Hutchins Paquette, 2nd ed. c 1997.
    Includes bibliographical references.
    ISBN 0-07-145542-6 (acid-free paper)
    1. Educational games.   2. Creative activities and seat work.   3. Critical thinking
—Study and teaching (Early childhood)—Activity programs.   4. Early childhood
education—Parent participation.   I. Paquette, Penny Hutchins.   II. Tuttle, Cheryl
Gerson. Thinking games to play with your child.   III. Title.

    LB1029.G3T88   2004   2005003486

1 2 3 4 5 6 7 8 9 0   FGR/FGR   0 9 8 7 6 5

ISBN 0-07-145542-6

McGraw-Hill books are available at special quantity discounts to use as premiums and sales
promotions, or for use in corporate training programs. For more information, please write to
the Director of Special Sales, Professional Publishing, McGraw-Hill, Two Penn Plaza, New York,
NY 10121-2298. Or contact your local bookstore.

This book is printed on acid-free paper.

To Cameron, Jared, and Braden
—C.T.

To Ben, Carlyn, Jack, Sam, Natalie, Mark, and Michael
—P.P.

AaBbCcDdEeFfGgHhIiJjKkLlMmNnOoPpQqRrSsTtUuVvWwXxYyZz

Contents

4 ■ Count Me In: Helping Your Child Develop Math Skills   107

5 ■ What? Helping Your Child Develop Memory Strategies   147

Acknowledgments

e would like to thank Nomi Isak Kleinmuntz, Judy Jacobi, Charles Gessner, Beverly Clark, Terry Pollack, Gayle Stoll, and Janina Murphy for their contributions. Meryl Sevinor, creator of Purple Pebble Games: Stepping Stones to Learning, was especially helpful with the phonemic awareness chapter.

Most of all we would like to express our gratitude to our children—Matthew, Ross, Eric, Danielle, and Michael—who grew up to be such thoughtful adults and helped us prove that the techniques in this book can work.

To the Thoughtful Parent

When Penny and I first published this book, we believed that playing games with children, interacting with them in positive ways, and becoming involved in their intellectual development at home would make a positive difference for our children. In the fourteen years since, more and more information has become available about learning and child development.

This information on how children learn to read confirmed our original beliefs. Parents can and should be involved in the development of their children. Reading to children, talking to them, and spending time with them will help their intellectual and emotional development.

Even though more statistical information supports the importance of active parenting, we know the job is the most challenging we will ever face. Besides being one of the most difficult professions, parenting is the one for which most of us have the least training. Between us, Penny and I have raised five children. Parenthood required us each to be teacher, psychologist, nurse, and coach. We did the best we could, but often we needed help. We called the doctor when we needed medical advice, and we talked to family and friends and looked to self-help books for assistance in the psychological areas. We expected teachers to teach our children all they needed to know to succeed in school, and we expected our children to learn.

When we sent our children off to school, we believed, as our parents did, that school could do everything necessary to give them the skills and confidence they would need to thrive and prosper in higher education and in the adult world. Both as parents and as teachers, we soon discovered we were wrong. The schools couldn't do it alone.

It became clear to us that children need extra support. My older son needed to work on his reading speed; my younger one needed help with his math facts. Both had terrible handwriting. Penny's children had trouble with reading comprehension and book reports. Before long, we realized the classroom teacher did not have the time to give them all the special attention they would need. And that was nearly thirty years ago.

Today's School Day

Today, the situation is even more difficult. When we were growing up, the entire school day could be devoted to teaching the basics. But now, new problems reduce the number of hours teachers can spend on the development of foundation-level skills. Budget woes are increasing class size, and the teaching day is fragmented by a multitude of offerings that are essential in today's society. In many local public school systems, a portion of every day is spent on important topics such as sex education, drug education, self-esteem development, computer literacy, and crisis intervention. Of course, all these offerings are invaluable, but they also take important time away from developing the basics of reading, writing, math, and the application skills that I call thinking skills.

During a typical day in our school system, children are in school for six hours. Fortunately, the school day continues to offer important enrichment activities, including gym, art, and music. Like many school systems, ours also offers special events and self-esteem development programs. Children spend nearly an hour eating lunch and playing at recess. With these activities, almost half the day is already spoken for. During the three hours left, teachers are expected to teach reading, writing, math facts, problem-solving skills, basic geography, and at least some science. Times have changed. Classroom teachers can't do it all. They need help.

As parents and teachers, we recognized the difference involved parents can make in their child's education. When you read to your child, you automatically improve his vocabulary. When you review homework, you show by your attention that learning is important. But if your family is anything like mine was, finding time to squeeze in one more activity is the ultimate challenge.

If the academic day is fragmented, most family days are even more splintered. Often, both parents work outside the home, and many families are managed by single parents. You work, you shop, you do laundry, you fix meals, and you may even manage to give a portion of your day to a volunteer project. Even if your children watch a lot of television and at times seem tethered to their computer games, they aren't exactly idle. They are playing soccer and baseball and softball and football. They go to dance class and piano lessons.

They have paper routes and dentist appointments, Cub Scout or Brownie meetings. You may recognize the need for at-home academic support but perhaps can't find the time or energy to accomplish one more thing during the day.

When I talk to parents during parent-teacher conferences, they are eager to do what they can to help their children learn, but they are also frustrated. In addition to having limited time, they often find that their children are not terribly cooperative.

The frustrations are predictable. Children do not view their parents as their teachers. When I tried to help my children with their homework, they were quick to tell me I didn't do it the way their teachers did, and that my way must be wrong. Penny had similar experiences.

And, as parents, we have to acknowledge that children would rather work on improving their laser-blasting skills than their classroom skills. Children do not want their parents to take what they perceive as precious time away from their favorite television program or computer game. After an afternoon of homework, they don't want to do more "work" on reading, and they aren't too excited about practicing those math facts.

When my oldest was encouraged to practice his reading at home, he hid his books behind the radiator. Homework became a struggle, and our working together created a tension that was not helpful for either of us. My ego was tied to his learning and his academic achievement, and I got angry when I felt he wasn't trying hard enough. We usually ended our homework sessions shouting at each other. This wasn't the way I had visualized the "enrichment time."

Of course, some schools have managed to offer enrichment programs within the school day—what many schools call gifted or talented programs. But what if your child, the one you know has many gifts and a multitude of talents, doesn't quite fit into your school system's definition of gifted? What if those programs offer other children the opportunity to go beyond the traditional curriculum and learn to integrate what they have learned, the opportunity to develop those essential thinking skills? Or what if your child needs a little extra time or help? Where does that leave your child? It leaves her out.

And where does that leave you, as a parent? It leaves you angry and frustrated. And to make matters worse, you feel guilty because you don't think you have the time or the expertise to help.

The good news is that you are wrong. The primary goals of *Thinking Games for Kids* are to help you maximize your child's enthusiasm for learning, to create a desire for him to practice skills and continue learning, and to help him feel good about himself. And that is not as difficult as you may think.

What Can Parents Do?

I originally designed the activities in this book to help my own boys learn the basics and to improve their images of themselves as learners. My first attempts were not as successful as I had hoped. When I began to use these activities, they looked too much like schoolwork and were quickly rejected. It was not until I "packaged" them so they looked more like commercial games that I was able to capture their interest. Children like to play games. I recognized that and used it to my advantage.

Then my children enjoyed that special time with me. We had fun. They looked forward to playing, and they became excited about learning. I was thrilled with our success. I introduced some of my ideas to Penny and we pooled our experiences as parents and educators to help you have the same positive learning experiences with your child.

We know you can make a difference. Researchers tell us parents are an important resource. In its book, *What Works: Research About Teaching and Learning*, the U.S. Department of Education states, "Parents are their children's first and most influential teachers." The writers of this report further explain that parents have the opportunity to do things at home that will help their children succeed at school, but parents are doing less than they might. Their research has shown that mothers spend, on average, less than half an hour each day talking, explaining, and/or reading to their children. Fathers, on average, spend less than fifteen minutes.

I'm sure you want to spend more time than average, but you may need guidance and direction. The activities and strategies in this book will provide you with tools to help your child strengthen the skills she is learning at school. The games will improve thinking skills, provide structured activities that are both educational and fun, and help you and your child feel good about yourselves.

The self-esteem of young children is fragile and needs to be nurtured. The games themselves won't miraculously improve self-esteem, but they will provide you with a way to give positive messages to your child.

If your child knows there will be a time set aside when you will be together, you are showing him he is important and that you want to be with him. Because these games are organized so that there is more than one way to win—by points, by creativity, and/or by chance—there are many opportunities for praise and positive reinforcement. We all like to hear good things about ourselves, and when the words are said often enough by someone we trust, we begin to believe what we hear.

Most of the games in this book are intended for children in preschool through third grade. However, we recognize that older children like to play, too. In this new edition, we have included instructions for adapting the games or the rules of the games, so it is easy to include older children as well.

Why This Book?

As with the previous edition, Chapters 2 through 4 offer games that enhance reading, writing, and arithmetic skills—the three Rs. In this revised edition, Chapter 1 starts with the newest research in reading readiness—what reading specialists call *phonemic awareness*. Experts now believe that an emphasis on the individual sounds (phonemes) of spoken language helps better prepare our children to understand the connection between the spoken word and the written word. What parents and teachers long suspected was an important component in learning to read is now visible, as functional magnetic resonance imaging (fMRI) technology allows us to watch the human brain as it learns new words. This new technology provides us with concrete evidence about learning to read, and we now know that process can begin long before children learn their ABCs. The first chapter introduces the skills that experts believe are the best predictors for reading success.

The final chapter focuses on an equally important R: remembering. We present games in this chapter to help your child develop the strategies necessary for remembering everything from the name of a classmate to the facts of a social studies assignment.

Each game in the book includes a discussion of the skills developed while playing, directions for playing the game, the materials needed, the amount of time to allow for play, adaptations for older children, and suggestions for variations. Under the "Number of Players" heading, the numbers include a parent unless otherwise indicated. By reading the "How to Play" section, you can determine whether the activity is appropriate for your child. The "Hints and

Variations" section will provide you with expanded guidelines for play, so you can modify the games to fit your family. Personalized variations will add to your enjoyment while improving your child's self-esteem and thinking skills.

Of course, every child is different, but all benefit from attention and validation. It is important to remember that how your child learns can be even more important than what he learns.

What Brain Research Tells Us

As researchers have learned more and more about how children learn, we can take advantage of that information. We know a lot more about how the brain works, and we have come to appreciate the importance of the connectors, called neurons, that help process information within the brain. With the help of neurotransmitters, these connectors—some researchers estimate there are forty quadrillion (40 followed by fifteen zeros) possible connections—send and receive messages and power the process that helps us learn.

According to John Ratey, in *A User's Guide to the Brain*, these neural connections are stimulated, expanded, and strengthened when we take part in activities that challenge our brains. As we challenge children with activities that strengthen a specific skill, the number and strength of neural connections devoted to that skill are improved. The good news is that brains selectively strengthen the connections that are used. The bad news is that those left idle die off. This neurological activity continues throughout our lives, but opportunities for strengthening and growth appear to be the most pronounced between the ages of two and eleven. What an opportunity for parents! We can take advantage of this window of opportunity to provide neurological "strength training."

We know that children are born with the biological capabilities for learning. We also know that, as the brain is challenged, it stretches to form new connections. These new connections make learning easier. Once a particular subject is mastered and stored in the lower areas of our brains, it becomes hardwired into our long-term memory. When this happens, neurons once engaged in the learning activity can move on to new challenges.

While the biological component is important, emotions cannot be underestimated. When children enjoy what they are learning, they are willing to devote more time to it. And nothing improves skills like practice. When children are actively engaged in playing, the connections get stronger. When they are successful, their motivation to learn is further enhanced. As a parent, you can create an environment where creative thinking flourishes.

Why These Games Work

It doesn't take a lot of time to help your child engage in thoughtful play that strengthens the connections in the brain. The activities in this book are designed to give the maximum benefit in the minimum amount of time. Some take only minutes to play, require no special materials, and may be taken up at the spur of the moment.

We have also attacked one of the other stumbling blocks to our success in helping our own children. When my children were younger, most of the games they wanted to play were not enjoyable to me as an adult. Most were too repetitive; they did not use thinking skills creatively; they were too long; and someone always felt like a loser. I hated going around the same game board over and over again. So I planned activities that challenged the children and me, with an emphasis on creativity and humor. If I wanted to play with the children, the games would have to be fun for all of us.

Together, Penny and I have taken these early experiences and created games that all families can enjoy. These activities teach new skills, enhance old ones, and best of all, don't feel like work. They use basic skills in new and different ways every time each game is played. The prereading, reading, and writing activities develop language skills that help children make themselves understood. While playing the math games, your child will use math facts not only to arrive at a sum or a remainder, but also to make judgments about his immediate world and to arrive at logical conclusions. Because strategy is an important part of all the games, your child will develop strong thinking and problem-solving skills.

These games accept the fact that most children enjoy competition but ensure that the enjoyment of playing is more important than winning or losing. (If competition is stressful for your child, you don't have to keep score.) Remember, winning does not necessarily mean someone else has to lose. We need to think of winning as the accomplishment of an objective—a goal reached.

The activities allow enough variation in rules so children of different ages can play with parents at the same time. You can encourage your children to use their imaginations and their creativity in picking materials for some of the games or in making variations in the playing style. Children who enjoy playing commercial games may even create their own game boards from a shirt cardboard or a file folder. They may add bonus or penalty squares to introduce the element of chance. Redirect their computer activities and have them find images that can be used in the games. The choice is theirs.

You will need no special knowledge to play. You don't have to know phonics or algorithms. You need only be open to new ideas. It is important to use your child's knowledge as a base to build on. If your child is just starting to recognize beginning and ending sounds in words, encourage her to play the games that will strengthen those skills. If she has a basic understanding of math facts but needs some drill work, guide her toward a game that makes strengthening memory skills fun. Be sure to reward creative behavior, and your child will begin to view learning as an exciting and self-rewarding activity.

You can provide a rich environment and a variety of activities to stimulate your child's imagination. As Albert Einstein said, "Imagination is more important than knowledge, for knowledge is limited, whereas imagination embraces the entire world." Allow your child to be directly involved in choosing the activity and interpreting the rules. Play with your child and show her that learning, at any age, can be fun. You will plant a seed and watch your child grow in self-esteem, curiosity, creativity, and independence.

The games also help alleviate guilt. Sure, we would all like to have the time to pack our children in the car once or twice a week to see the latest exhibit at a science museum, children's museum, or art museum. That's just not always possible. We may not have a lot of time, but we can make the most of the time we have. We can enrich our children's lives in short bursts when we recognize that that time is valuable to a child's development. We can do something at home that is challenging, productive, and creative. Because the activities require no special materials or use materials found around the house (newspapers, cards, kitchen items), the games can begin spontaneously.

These activities don't expect you to be a teacher in the classroom sense. Instead, they help you find ways to interact with your child as a parent who loves her and wants to enjoy her company. The activities teach that learning never stops, no matter how old you are.

Tips for Getting Started

If your child is resistant, don't force the games on him. Try to determine why he does not want to play. Is he afraid he will lose, or is he embarrassed to be playing where his friends might see him? Is he unsure of his ability with words or numbers, or does he just want to be someplace else? All of these issues exist at some time and must be taken into consideration. If you still cannot get him involved, postpone the activity. Try again at the dinner table or at the breakfast table, but don't get upset if he won't take the bait. Sometimes the best way to engage a reluctant child is to play during those long periods of waiting, especially in the car. If your child is a reluctant participant, browse through the book and find the games that can be played without any special materials. Then you have the opportunity to play a game, and your child won't even know it. Making sentences from license plate letters, playing with license numbers, and creating wordplay derived from street signs gives your child something to do during that boring car time. Once he has enjoyed the games in that environment, he may be less reluctant to play at home.

Remember, these games are designed to increase fun times with your child, not to produce tension.

When working with your child on academic skills, you can use the same approach as you would in teaching him a sport. A child learns to pitch a baseball or ride a bike by practicing with his parent. You point out technique, discuss strategy, act as a role model, and praise the child at every opportunity as he gets closer to the goal you both have set. You work toward establishing good habits.

The time you set aside may be as individual as the game you choose to play. It is important to choose a time when you are full of energy and enthusiasm. If you are an evening person, try the time right after dinner. If you are a morning person, you can play parts of these games at the breakfast table or on Saturday morning. But if your best time coincides with your child's favorite cartoon, postpone your game time.

Also consider your child's best learning time. Passive or hostile learners rarely absorb much. It would be ideal if both you and your child had the same high-energy time, but that is rarely the case. My sons were both grouchy in the morning—my best time. They would hardly talk, much less answer questions. It was hard enough to find out what they wanted for lunch! This was not a good time to try to play games. When they refused to get involved in the morning, I had to be the one to compromise, at least until they were more interested in and enthusiastic about the activities.

To get my sons started, I offered an extension of their bedtime with the understanding that we would use the time to play a game together. We agreed to complete at least one round. The first time we played a game, I assembled the necessary materials and determined where we would play: the kitchen table. One boy sat back with his arms crossed over his chest, and the other insisted on sitting in my lap. I said a two-word sentence, and they had to add words to make complete sentences. When they finally responded, the sentences were silly, and they made us laugh. The sillier the sentences became, the more involved the boys were. They even forgot to keep score. After the agreed-upon fifteen minutes of play, they wanted to continue, and the next night, they asked to play the game again. It had worked!

As they became familiar with the games, they began to choose their favorites, usually the ones they felt they had a good chance of winning. My greatest pleasure came when they began to see the possibilities for play at other times of the day or when a question from one of the games could be thrown out at any time and everyone would get involved in an abbreviated version of the game.

One of my boys was better at reading, and the other was good at math. Sometimes I could get them both to participate if they knew we would have time for both a reading and a math activity. Other times, only one of them would play while the other watched. Each avoided the chance of losing to his brother. This was OK. Fun is usually contagious, and even if they were not pulled into the game, they learned by watching.

All of the games are designed to be open-ended. The "rules" are given as guidelines to play. Feel free to vary the rules and the method of scoring if they do not fit your child or your immediate situation.

These games were built on flexibility and can only be enhanced by variation.

Keep in mind that when you play these games with your family, everyone is a winner. As your child grows in confidence and ability, she will develop the creative and critical thinking skills for success in the classroom and at home. Your family will grow closer with each opportunity to share a common activity, one that is specifically designed to be stimulating for both adults and children. Together you're embarking on a special adventure that provides a nurturing combination of love, learning, and laughter. Enjoy!

1

AaBbCcDdEeFfGgHhIiJjKkLlMmNnOoPpQqRrSsTtUuVvWwXxYyZz

Hear, Hear

Helping Your Child Develop Phonemic Awareness Skills

hen we help our children develop reading skills, we give them a great gift: a facility with language. Not only will they have the ability to learn, recall, and share information, which is useful and important in the classroom, but they will also develop a sense of self-esteem that they will carry with them through their school years and into their adult lives. Children with strong verbal skills and a solid foundation in reading are ready to succeed in the classroom, and that success will prepare them for the increasingly complex world in which we live.

Research indicates that the early school years are the most formative in a child's learning; 80 percent of a child's measurable intelligence is developed by the age of eight. We know, too, that this is the time when children grow in their self-esteem, cultural identity, independence, and ability to deal with the world around them. It is also a time when they need to develop a fascination with learning and with words. They must learn to manipulate written and spoken language—that is, to read and write—if they are to master their world and become independent adults. And the process must begin when they are very young.

Imagine yourself in a foreign country, say, China. You do not understand the language. Not only are you unable to read the signs, you don't even recognize the letters of the alphabet. How would you survive?

The situation is not that different for your very young child. But eventually, she recognizes your words and learns to mimic them. With time, her mimicry begins to have meaning. She begins to recognize that spoken words are made up of individual sounds (phonemes) and enjoys playing with those sounds. As you read to her, she realizes that the printed word has meaning, too. She begins to realize that those symbols on the page represent the sounds she hears when she speaks, and the magic of reading begins.

As she learns to read, write, and think clearly, her communication skills become a strength. The ability to make herself understood gives her confidence.

When most of us think of reading and reading readiness, we think of beginning with letter recognition and the ability to sound out unfamiliar words. While recognizing letters and associating them with the corresponding letter sound are essential in the development of reading, we need to consider an even earlier and equally important step in the development of reading skills: understanding that words are composed of sounds.

Most reading specialists today recognize the importance of understanding the sounds of spoken language before working with the printed letters of words. They know that training a young child to recognize the individual sounds—phonemes—in spoken words before he goes to school significantly improves his success in learning to read. The English language contains only forty-four of these phonemes, but combinations of them create all the words in the language.

As parents, we know that most young children learn to speak and respond to spoken language without any specific instruction. However, that is not enough. Yes, they need to understand the language of speech in order to read, but they also need to understand the code of speech as well. Before they can understand the meaning of the written word, they need to understand the structure of the word and to know that spoken words are actually made up of smaller individual sounds. Unless children have this basic understanding, printed symbols—letters—are meaningless.

Researchers today call this sound perception *phonemic awareness*, and leading educators now believe that this ability to hear and work with the sounds in words is an essential prereading skill. Once children can understand that spoken words are actually made up of smaller, individual sounds, they can associate those sounds with the printed symbols. This skill is considered so important that one highly regarded reading researcher, Keith Stanovich, has stated that phonemic awareness is the best predictor of the ease of early reading acquisition—even better than a child's IQ. Most reading specialists agree with him.

Many young children can develop this prereading skill quite easily when they are exposed to both spoken and written language. They learn it best through playful practice and fun. Therefore, reading to your child and having fun with words are the best ways to help your child develop an understanding and appreciation of the sounds of language.

The games in this section are designed to give you ideas for playing with language and helping your children develop phonemic awareness. Language, even the most complex, is made up of individual sounds, and since early reading development starts with an understanding of sounds, that's the focus of these games. In these games, an individual sound or phoneme is represented like this: /m/. Remember, the symbol does not represent the letter *m*, but rather the sound it makes: "mmmmmm," the beginning sound in *mop*, *man*, *mom*, and *mouse*. Later in the chapter, we provide games that help develop letter recognition skills, but in the beginning, the emphasis is on individual sounds and the blending of individual sounds.

You don't have to be a teacher to play these games. Phonemic awareness sounds technical, but it is not. Reading specialists indicate that phonemic awareness is made up of the following skills:

■ The ability to recognize individual sounds, including rhymes
■ The ability to produce individual sounds and rhymes (as you already do when you play with nursery rhymes)
■ The understanding that spoken language and individual words are made up of a series of sounds and that sentences are made up of a series of words (as you demonstrate when you are talking and reading to your child)
■ The ability to recognize specific sounds at the beginning, middle, and end of words and, later, the ability to produce words that have specific sounds at the beginning, the middle, or the end (as you practice when you talk about the sound at the beginning or end of your child's name)
■ An understanding that words can be broken down into individual sounds—for example, showing that the sounds /b/ /a/ /t/ can be blended to make a word, *bat*
■ An understanding that individual sounds can be removed from a word to create a new word—remove the /b/, and you are left with *at*
■ An understanding that words can be made up of several other words—cow/boy, for example
■ The alphabetic principle, which says that specific sounds are associated with specific letters of the alphabet

The games in this section are designed to develop and strengthen those specific areas. While wordplay has always been considered a fun activity, today we know that wordplay can make a significant contribution to reading readiness. These games put the emphasis precisely where it belongs, on the *play* part of wordplay. As with all the games in this book, skills develop as a result of having a good time.

The games with the earliest levels of skill development appear first. Although these games can help your preschool child develop reading readiness, phonemic awareness skills can continue to develop through the elementary grades. These games provide excellent reinforcement for children who have already begun to read.

Although most parents help their children learn the letters of the alphabet, recent research shows that it is essential to teach children not only the name of the letter, but also the sound the letter makes. This helps children associate the phoneme sound with letters, thereby recognizing that the written word is a symbolic representation of the spoken word. This is an essential component of learning to read. The games at the end of the chapter help children learn the sounds associated with letters of the alphabet.

Phonemic awareness and alphabetic awareness will help your children learn to read. You can help your children achieve these skills by simply playing games with them. Your enthusiasm for wordplay will rub off on them as you laugh along with them. So choose a game, and start having fun.

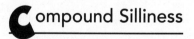

Compound Silliness

Purpose: This game helps your child understand that words can be made up of smaller units of words, that sounds can be added to or taken away from words to make new words, and that playing with words can be fun.

Materials Needed: This game can be played without materials. However, pictures of different items might help your child come up with target words, especially the first time you play the game. Paper and crayons may be used for a variation of the game.

Number of Players: 2 to 6

Time: Each round will take 5 to 10 minutes, depending upon the number of players.

How to Play: The object of the game is to create compound words from two small words and to have a good time in the process. Each player, in turn, says two words. The next player creates a compound word using the two words presented. For example, the first player might say "boy, foot." The next player would say "boyfoot" or "footboy" and then must describe what a boyfoot or footboy is. The other players also try to come up with a silly description, and the best description is decided by a vote of the players. The player with the best description gets a point, and the one with the most points at the end of the time played is the winner. Nonsense words are highly encouraged in this game, and creativity is rewarded.

Modifications for Older Children: Even older children can enjoy an opportunity to get silly. Since you are making nonsense words, older children do not have an advantage in this game. They can, however, use their more developed vocabulary to come up with more outrageous word choices. This is an opportunity to help them explore their creativity and see how wordplay can be fun. Often, older children like to have the opportunity to help younger children develop their skills. This game can put them in a position to excel and assist, an ideal combination for learning.

Hints and Variations: If there is time and interest, each player could draw a picture of what the new object is. Penny's grandchildren especially enjoy this variation. Keep paper and crayons ready when you play this as well as other games. Encourage the players to draw as many of the game answers as possible. It is important to keep a sense of playfulness with all of the activities, and funny pictures usually generate laughter. Allowing time to draw keeps the game informal and gives those who might be better at drawing a chance to excel.

Skills Developed: One of the early phonemic awareness skills is the ability to recognize that words can be combined to create new words. Compound words provide a good example of this concept because of the rich pictures they can bring to mind. Practice in breaking down and combining words leads to understanding that the words can be taken apart. As your child plays with these words, her skills develop, and she learns that she can sound out words she doesn't recognize. She needs to learn to break words into parts before she can learn to break them into syllables. Compound Silliness gives your child practice making words of more than one part. As she creates compound words, she will be developing the awareness that words are made up of parts, and this will provide the foundation for breaking words up into their individual phonemes.

Clap Time

Purpose: In this game your child will learn to count the number of words in a sentence, which will help when learning to hear the number of sounds in a word.

Materials Needed: No materials are required for this game.

Number of Players: 2 to 4

Time: Allow 5 to 10 minutes for each round of play.

How to Play: The first player says a two-word sentence and claps for each word in the sentence. The next player must say a three-word sentence, also clapping for each word. For example, if the first sentence is *Kids play* (two claps), the next sentence might be, *I like dolls* (three claps). The next sentence could be *The sun is blue* (four claps). Play continues with each player giving a sentence containing one more word than the previous sentence until a player cannot come up with a sentence of the correct length. As in *The sun is blue*, the sentences don't have to make sense. The last player to give a sentence correctly is the winner.

Modifications for Older Children: When playing with older children, you can incorporate some of their schoolwork. If you do it this way, the sentences will need to be realistic. If they are working on parts of a sentence, have them use nouns, verbs, adjectives, and adverbs appropriately. You can also limit their sentences to a particular subject they are studying. If they have homework on states and capitals, their sentences would have to relate to information about states. With this modification, your child will get the added benefit of reinforcement in the content area.

Hints and Variations: When you model for this game, use only one-syllable words. If your child is using words with more than one syllable, that is OK, but make sure he claps only once for the word and does not clap out the syllables.

The object is to help your child identify individual words, not syllables. You can have a lot of fun with this game if you keep it silly. Remember, meaning is not important if the words make up a sentence, with a beginning, middle, and end. This is also a good way to make your child aware of words like *the*, *a*, and *and* as important words in a sentence.

Skills Developed: One of the first steps in phonemic awareness is to understand that sentences are made up of words. It is easier to hear the number of words in a sentence or the number of syllables in a word than the number of sounds in a word—the skill you are hoping to get to. Activities that involve counting the number of words in a sentence or the number of syllables in a word are the beginning steps toward learning to isolate the individual sounds in a word.

Rhyme Time

Purpose: This game helps your child understand that words can rhyme and end with the same sounds. The game will also help build vocabulary.

Materials Needed: No materials are needed, so you can play anywhere. Play while waiting for a doctor's appointment or while waiting for your food in a restaurant.

Number of Players: 2 to 6

Time: Each turn takes less than 5 minutes and can be played any time you are together with children and nothing else is going on.

How to Play: The object of this game is for players to come up with words that rhyme with a clue word. One player names a clue word, one that has rhyming possibilities. Each player, in turn, names another word that rhymes with the clue word. For example, if the clue word is *bear*, players might think of *wear*, *tear*, *fair*, *care*, *share*, *stare*, and *mare*. If one player is unable to answer, she can forfeit her turn, and the next player can respond. If the play continues around, the player who forfeited will receive another chance. The last player to name a rhyming word chooses the clue word for the next round.

Modifications for Older Children: Older children can participate in this simple game because it involves creativity in coming up with words that rhyme. You can increase the difficulty level for your older child by requiring her to use only words with more than one syllable. This will stretch her thinking and expose your younger child to the concept that words can be broken into syllables.

Hints and Variations: This is a particularly good game for your younger child. Since preschools and kindergartens spend a lot of time with rhyming, it will give her a chance to show off at home what she has learned at school, and will ease frustrations she may feel with the more difficult games older siblings might like to play. Success at these early-level games builds confidence and can improve self-esteem.

This is also a time to have fun with words. You can change the game so that the rhyming words have to be nonsense words only (for example, rhymes for *dog* would be *mog, wog, gog,* etc.), or you can include nonsense words with real words once there are no more or you can no longer think of any real words that rhyme with the targeted word. Our grandchildren particularly enjoy coming up with nonsense rhymes for their names—*Sam* and *blam,* for example.

You might also begin collecting pictures of objects that rhyme— a picture of a mitten and a kitten, a cat and a hat, a tree and a bee, for example. Mix up the pictures, and ask your child to find the matching rhymes. Or have your child look for rhyming words in catalogs or magazines. This makes it a little easier, as your child will not have to come up with words on her own.

Skills Developed: One of the early skills developed on the way to phonemic awareness is a recognition that words can rhyme. Rhyming provides your child with a way to compare and contrast the sounds in words. As she learns to read, your child needs to be able understand and hear that some words end with the same group of sounds (rhyme). Once she knows that the combination of the sounds /a/ and /t/ creates a chunk of a word and makes the sound /at/, she can sound out words such as *cat, bat, rat,* and so on. We use this skill throughout our lives as we associate unfamiliar words with similar words that we already know. One of the methods we use to pronounce unfamiliar words is to break them down by syllable and look for familiar patterns. It provides an additional framework for attacking the unknown.

Bequeath could be a very difficult word if we didn't already know the word *beneath*.

This activity encourages your child to become more alert to her environment, because she needs to think of objects that fit the rhyming sequence of the game. She will begin to see new relationships between words and will understand and apply the rules of rhyming.

Beginnings

Purpose: This game helps your child see that words can begin with the same sound. It then helps children produce words to show that they understand the concept. It also helps build vocabulary.

Materials Needed: No materials are needed to play this game, so it can be played anywhere, at any time. Use it any time you can—while cooking dinner, riding in a car, waiting in a restaurant, walking down the street.

Number of Players: 2 to 6

Time: Each turn takes less than 5 minutes, so this is a good spur-of-the-moment activity.

How to Play: The object of this game is for players to find objects that begin with the same sound. One player chooses a letter sound and announces it to the group. Each player, in turn, names something in the immediate area that begins with that sound. The winner is the last one to find an object with the selected beginning sound. For example, while walking down the street, the first player chooses the sound /r/ and says the word *rock*. The next player says "roof." Play continues until no player is able to see an object that begins with /r/. At that point, the round is over, and the person who named the last object is the winner.

Modifications for Older Children: This is a good game for including older children. Even complicated words start with one sound. If you are playing the game by looking for items in your immediate area, children of all ages can be challenged by looking for objects. If you are playing using the hints and variations, encourage your older children to use words from school texts or homework. This helps reinforce concepts as they work with more sophisticated words.

Hints and Variations: Instead of finding the objects in the area, the players can also develop vocabulary by simply naming any word they can think of that begins with the beginning sound. You can extend the playing time of the game and reinforce the concept by drawing pictures of words that begin with the selected sound. You could even develop your own alphabet book.

Skills Developed: The game helps develop skills on many levels. It helps children listen for and isolate the smallest units of our spoken language, the phonemes, and it helps them find the sound in one of the easiest places, the beginning of the word. It helps them hear how different words can begin with the same sound and shows them how to listen for the similarities in words. The ability to group words by the beginning sound is also one method of categorizing and organizing information. It provides a framework for logical thinking. Because this game has no written component, it will encourage your child to be more attentive to his environment and will help him build a longer attention span. Both of these skills are needed throughout school years and in almost any job situation.

 **S**tart Up

Purpose: This game helps your child understand that words are made up of a series of sounds and that the words can be broken up into individual phonemes or sounds. Like the previous game, it encourages children to isolate the sound at the beginning of a word.

Materials Needed: No materials are needed to play this game. It can be played anywhere there are objects to see, so play it any time you can—while walking down the street or cleaning the playroom, or combined with a trip to a playground.

Number of Players: 2 to 6

Time: Each turn takes less than 5 minutes, so this game can be played at the spur of the moment anytime you want a fun activity.

How to Play: The object of this game is for the players to discover and identify a secret word. One player begins by selecting an object in the immediate area and revealing only the beginning sound of the word. For example, if the object is a ball, the player would say it begins with the sound /b/. The other players must guess the secret object by naming objects they see that begin with that sound. The first player to guess the object is the winner.

If the players are having a difficult time discovering the object, they may ask yes-and-no questions in order to determine its location and use. For example, they may ask, "Is someone wearing it? Is it on the floor? Can I hold it in my hand?" If your child is not quite sure how to ask yes or no questions, you should take the first turn and explain how you are arriving at your secret word and the beginning sound.

Modifications for Older Children: This is a good game to use with children of many ages. Older children who already know how to isolate beginning sounds may be the selector and come up with the chosen word and sound. All ages can play because there is no limit to the words chosen. Older children are often more creative with their choices. One of Cheryl's favorite examples was her son's choice of her contact lens for the beginning sound /l/.

Hints and Variations: This game can be difficult for younger children if they do not know how to isolate the beginning sound from the rest of a word. They might need some examples from you before the game begins. You can also use names of the people playing or friends at school instead of objects.

If it is too difficult, you or an older child may need to be the selector until your child starts to understand the concept. You might also need to help your younger child figure out how to ask the identifying questions.

Skills Developed: One of the first stages of phonemic awareness is for your child to understand that words can begin with the same sound and then for your child to be able to produce the words that do so. When he learns that words can share the same sounds, he will later expand that knowledge when he sees that words can also share the same series of letters. It is easier for him to hear and compare the sounds when they are at the beginning and end of words, so it is important to start the awareness at the beginning-sound level. Start Up requires your child to identify and isolate the beginning sound in order to pick the secret word he wants to use. He will have to choose an object, think about how it starts, and then voice the sound at the beginning without saying the rest of the word. This is a skill that goes before being able to sound out the whole word that he comes across when he begins to read.

ound Bingo

Purpose: This is another game that helps your child understand that words are made up of a series of sounds and that the words can be broken up into individual phonemes or sounds. It encourages children to isolate the sound at the beginning of a word but provides a picture cue to make the task a little easier.

Materials Needed: For this game you will need to create bingo-type cards on which each of the squares contains an object, and the objects begin with different sounds. When you are playing with children in preschool, each child should use a card of no more than six squares. You can increase the number of squares as your child starts school and becomes more familiar with the skills. You will also need tokens or squares of blank paper to cover the pictures that correspond to the sounds called. The caller will need a bag with tiles labeled with individual letters. You can create these yourself or use game pieces from another game, such as Scrabble.

Number of Players: 4 or more (including 1 player who is the caller and does not compete)

Time: Allow 5 minutes for rounds using a smaller number of squares. The game might take up to 10 minutes when you use cards with more pictures.

How to Play: Each child has a bingo-type card containing pictures that begin with different sounds. The caller (you or your older child until the younger children are more proficient at this skill) pulls a letter from a bag and says the sound made by that letter. The other players must cover the picture that begins with that sound. The play continues until one child has covered all the pictures on her card. The caller then can uncover the pictures on the winning card and say the name of the picture and the name of the beginning sound in order to reinforce the skill.

Modifications for Older Children: Your older child can be a leader in this game, as the caller has to be able to identify the letters with the sounds they make. Although your older child may already have good phonemic awareness, this type of repetition can only strengthen her skills. As long as the letters are picked from the bag in a random order and the pictures on the cards represent a large number of sound choices, the game will be fair and fun for all ages.

Hints and Variations: It can be fun to make the individual bingo cards. You can use pictures from magazines, draw the pictures, or download them from your computer. You might pick a category for each card, such as animals or toys or foods, so that your child can have fun picking a different category card each time or choose his favorite category. For younger children, use only the consonant sounds, as they are much easier to hear than the vowels.

This game can be played using the ending sounds and eventually the middle sounds of the words also. This variation makes the game more difficult because it is easier to hear that *dog* starts with /d/ than that it ends with /g/ or that the middle sound is /o/. Use this variation as your child gains skill in isolating the sounds in words.

Skills Developed: Children need a lot of practice isolating the sounds in words. Since this is such an important foundation for beginning phonemic awareness and then reading, it is a skill that needs practice in a variety of ways. When your child learns to isolate the sound at the beginning of a word, you can move on to sounds at the end of the word and in the middle of the word. This experience will help children as they begin to sound out words in order to read.

nap

Purpose: This game helps build automaticity in identifying the sounds at the beginning and end of words.

Materials Needed: You will need a deck of cards illustrated with pictures of common objects. The pictures should include many objects that begin or end with the same sound.

Number of Players: 2 to 4

Time: Allow 10 minutes to get through a deck.

How to Play: Place the deck of cards face down in front of the players, and turn over one card to start a second pile. Each player takes a turn drawing a card from the face-down pile and placing it in the face-up pile. When a newly drawn card has the same beginning sound as the top card in the face-up pile, the first child to identify the match by saying "snap" collects the pile. Play continues with the player who has the next turn, placing the top card in the face-up pile. The child with the most cards at the end of the deck is the winner.

Modifications for Older Children: Older children can also benefit from being able to quickly identify sounds in words. If your children can read, play this game using several sets of cards with individual letters of the alphabet. Playing this way reinforces the ability to quickly identify a letter and the sound it makes.

Hints and Variations: This game can be changed to one where the child must find similar ending sounds or middle sounds. Middle sounds are more difficult, and that type of identification might take longer for her to figure out. If the ages of your children are similar, it will make the game fairer.

Skills Developed: When your child is reading, it is important for her to be able to sound out unknown words quickly so that the meaning of the sentence is not lost. She must be able to read fluently in order to read accurately and with the proper expression. Fluency and automaticity are essential phonemic awareness skills needed to enhance comprehension. These skills are developed through practice and exposure. When your child is encouraged to come up with the desired sound quickly, she is reinforcing her ability to quickly identify the correct sound in a word.

orter

Purpose: This is another game to help your child hear that words are made up of sounds and locate those sounds in a word. It also helps children understand that words can belong to more than one category.

Materials Needed: For this game, you will need scissors and many colorful magazines. Catalogs and ad circulars from the newspaper also are great for this game. To prepare for the game, gather a large supply of pictures of as many things as possible. You can cut the pictures from the magazines, catalogs, and ad circulars or assemble miscellaneous cards from other games.

Number of Players: 2 to 4

Time: Actual play time should take up to 5 minutes per round.

How to Play: The object of this game is to create the largest pile of pictures in a particular category. First, determine the category you will be using for the sorting. You can use something that begins with the sound /d/ (or any other beginning sound). You could also categorize by a function (for example, something you play with, something you can eat). You could use a particular color or any other category that makes sense or fun.

Spread all of the pictures face up in front of the players. All players look through the pictures and select ones that fit the category. Collect all of the objects that start with /b/, for example, or all of the pictures that show people eating, or all of the pictures that are blue, and put them into a pile. When no more pictures can be taken, the player with the most pictures that fit the category wins.

Modifications for Older Children: This game requires quick thinking, and it might be unfair to include older children with younger children unless they play with different rules. If your children's ages are very different, you might want them to take turns selecting pictures so that the older child won't get more by virtue of the fact that he can think faster and has greater experience with categorization. (There can still be a winner because one player may need to pass for a turn if he can't find a picture to fit the category.) Once everyone is finished picking, there can be a final turn where all players get to look at the remaining pictures and have time to think about how each one could fit.

Hints and Variations: You can use the same pictures over and over again by just changing the category designation. It can be very creative because a particular picture might fit in more than one category designation. A picture of a dog would fit in the category of beginning sound /d/ because it is a dog, in the /l/ category because it has legs, and in the /p/ category because it is a pet. If your child can support his reason for putting the picture in the category, allow it to stand. In this way, you are encouraging creativity and flexible thinking as well as phonemic awareness.

This game can be made more challenging if you decide that each picture must satisfy two categories. For example, the items must be something you can eat and also be blue.

Skills Developed: This game develops different types of skills depending upon how it is played. When played so that the items are sorted by the sounds at the beginning, end, or middle of a word, Sorter helps your child isolate the sounds in a word—a crucial step in phonemic awareness. If Sorter is played so that the items are sorted by type, use, color, or some other category, it helps children understand how the pictured items are part of a larger category. This latter variation is not applying a phonemic awareness skill, but the practice in sorting will help with comprehension once your child learns to read. If you play Sorter so that the players place items in piles where they must satisfy more than one category designation, your child is learning to isolate attributes of a particular item—a skill that is important in math and science.

Sentence Silliness

Purpose: In this game, your child produces words that begin with a particular sound, which encourages him to show he understands that words are made up of sounds.

Materials Needed: No materials are required for this game.

Number of Players: Up to 6 (more fun with many players)

Time: Each round should take no more than 5 minutes.

How to Play: The goal of this game is to create a sentence where all words begin with the same sound—for example, *Smart, smiling, sensitive Sara Susan Smith sang silly songs sitting somewhere south since Sunday.* The first player starts with one word. The next player adds a word that begins with the same sound as the first word and makes a sentence. For example, the first player might say, "Feet." The next player would say, "Feet fly." The next player says, "Fred's feet fly," and so on. The play continues until no player can add a word to increase the sentence. The last player to add a word is the winner.

Modifications for Older Children: Since this game encourages silliness and fun, it is fun for all ages, and it can be played anywhere you are waiting—at a restaurant or in traffic. (Dads and moms can particularly enjoy this one.) You can make it a little more challenging for older children (and parents) by requiring them to use words of more than one syllable. It is also OK to play in a team with your younger child to help her come up with a word, since this skill is harder than just hearing the sound at the beginning of the word.

Hints and Variations: Encourage creativity when you play this game. Sentences should be as silly as possible. If your child does not understand how to make a sentence, you can change the game so that each player must come up with a descriptive word that begins with the same sound as a person's name, and each player gets a point for each description. For example, for Carol, descriptive words could be *calm, cool, colorful, cold*, etc. When playing with names, there is a danger that some words might hurt a child's feelings, so you can subtract a point for any hurtful words used.

Skills Developed: Once your child is able to identify the beginning sound of a word, the next step is to be able to say a word with that beginning sound. Sentence Silliness provides a way to get your child to say words with a particular sound, creating alliterations, without it seeming like drill. The idea is to have fun with words so that he will think of wordplay and reading as fun. This game also develops memory skills because each player must remember all the words in the sentence and repeat them as the new word is added. (You can help here because younger children will have difficulty remembering all the words.)

Fishing

Purpose: This game encourages your child to think of all the different parts of words: beginning, middle, and ending sounds, number of sounds, and number of syllables.

Materials Needed: You will need a deck of cards with pictures on them instead of numbers. You can make the deck by pasting pictures over the numbers on a regular deck or use a commercial deck from another game—cards from Old Maid or Go Fish, for example. Make sure the pictures are of familiar objects that your child knows and that everyone agrees on the identification. For example, players might have a card with a picture of a taxi on it. The players must agree that this card will be called a taxi, or a cab, or a car for the purposes of this game. It really doesn't matter what they choose to call it, as long as they agree.

Number of Players: 2 to 4

Time: Each game should take between 5 and 10 minutes.

How to Play: The goal of the game is to have the most pairs of cards at the end of play. Deal each player six cards, and place the remaining cards face down in a stack in the middle of the players. The first player looks at his cards and decides which one he would like to find a match for. He asks the other players if they have a card to match one of his and designates how he wants the match. For example, if the card he wants to match is a dog, he might ask if any other players have a card with one of the following properties: beginning with the /d/ sound, ending with the /g/ sound, with only one syllable, with three sounds, etc. The other players must look at all of their cards to see if any of the pictures meet the designation called for. If another player has a picture of a dish and the called-for designation was beginning with the /d/ sound, that player must give over the card, and the first player then has a match and places those cards face down in front of him. Play rotates, with each player having a turn to ask. If no player has a card that matches, the asking player draws a card from the pile in the middle, and play passes to the next player. Each player determines which designation he will ask for at each turn. When no more matches can be made, the player with the most matches is the winner.

Modifications for Older Children: Have your older child play the concentration variation of this game, described below, as it is the most challenging.

Hints and Variations: After playing this game for a while, the players should become familiar with the objects and their properties. Use the same cards, and create a concentration game where all cards are placed face down in rows, and each player turns over two, looking for a match. This is more difficult because normally children would be looking for an identical match. In this variation of concentration, they might find a dog and a duck. These match because they both begin with /d/. Before starting to play this way, one property should be designated for play—either beginning sound or ending sound works best for this game. The one with the most matches wins.

Skills Developed: The typical development of phonemic awareness skills includes the awareness that a word can be analyzed and that it shares properties with other words: it can rhyme with other words, can be divided into syllables, and has a beginning, middle, and ending sound. In this game, each player must analyze the words (pictures on the cards) as the player determines which properties to look for. Your child is encouraged to use his analytic skills as well as his skills in isolating the sounds and syllables in a word.

Sound It Out

Purpose: This game provides practice in separating words into parts (phonemes) and blending the sounds back together to discover the word.

Materials Needed: For this game, you will need small objects and toys and a bag to conceal the items. Use small objects, such as toy cars, toy trucks, baby-doll bottles, small spoons, etc., so that they can fit into a bag. (Plastic bags from the supermarket will work if you double the bag so that the players can't see the objects.)

Number of Players: 2 to 4

Time: Allow enough time to go through all the objects in the bag. Choose the number of objects according to how much time you have to play.

How to Play: Gather objects you have around the house, perhaps from other games. Have everyone say the names of the objects so all players will be calling them by the same name. This avoids confusion later. Place all the objects in the bag.

One player looks in the bag and holds one object in her hand. She tells the other players the sounds that make up the name of the object. For example, if the object is a doll, she would say /d/, /o/, /l/. The next player has to tell what the object is by blending the sounds to get the word *doll*. If that player can't guess, the next player has a chance, and so on. The player to guess the object gets 1 point. Players take turns holding an object, and play continues until all objects are used.

Modifications for Older Children: This game may be too easy for a child who is already reading well and may be frustrating for the younger child to play with someone who can do it easily. This would be a good game to play as partners if your children are of different ages. Your older and younger children can play against you, or you and the younger child can partner against the older child. Once the object is selected, have a secret conference to go over the sounds, and let the younger child say them to the other players.

Hints and Variations: As stated above, taking apart the sounds might be difficult for children in the early grades, but it is an important skill for them to learn. Allow variations in their ability to segment (take apart) the sounds. If they say /d/, /ol/ for doll, that should be acceptable until they can take apart the middle sound of the word. If your child can only give the beginning sound of the word, accept that also until she can break the word down further. You can practice with the items before you play, but that does not always guarantee she will be able to do as practiced until she really understands the skill. Remember to keep the emphasis on fun, and praise all efforts toward the goal of segmenting all of the sounds and blending them into a word.

Skills Developed: Once your child can isolate the beginning and ending and middle sounds in a word, she needs to be able to take the sounds apart and blend them together to reform the word. She needs to hear how to do this before she can sound out words in her reading. It will be easier for her to blend the sounds than to take them apart, but it is important to provide exposure and practice with both skills so that your child will begin to understand the logic of words.

Toss Down

Purpose: This game encourages your child to hear the beginning sound in a word and later to locate sounds in other parts of the word. It combines the sound with the letter that makes the sound. This print awareness is one of the final steps in reading preparation. This game also helps children see the sequence of the alphabet.

Materials Needed: For this game, you will need cards printed with all the letters of the alphabet in capital letters, one letter in the middle of each card. Assign a point value to each card, and write that at the bottom of the card. (Cardboard from shirts pressed at the cleaners is good for this purpose.) You will also need a beanbag or small stuffed animal (such as a Beanie Baby) that will not bounce.

Number of Players: 2 to 6

Time: Allow at least 10 minutes to give everyone many opportunities to play.

How to Play: Place the cards face up on the floor in rows that do not overlap. Make sure the cards are placed in alphabetical order. Each child in turn stands twelve inches away from the rows of cards and tosses the beanbag to land on a card. She then says a word that begins with the sound where the beanbag has landed. If she is correct, she gets the number of points at the bottom of the card. At the end of the time allotted, the one with the most points is the winner.

Modifications for Older Children: With older children, have them toss two beanbags and name a word that begins with one of the sounds and ends with the other. To score, they earn the point value of the card used for the beginning sound.

Hints and Variations: Once your child can easily state words with the beginning sounds, modify the game to require that each player name a word that ends with the sound on the card. When you are assigning point values to the cards, give more points to vowels, since they are harder to isolate at the beginning of a word than a consonant.

As younger children are learning the beginning sounds, you can simplify this game by using only a limited number of letters.

Skills Developed: One of the first phonemic awareness skills is hearing the beginning sound in a word. One of the last steps is to understand that the sound is represented by a particular letter. This game provides practice in coming up with words that begin or end with the sound a particular *letter* makes.

This game also involves movement and a sensory cue. When your child holds the beanbag to throw it on the card, she uses more than one sense. Brain research has shown that combining movement and involving more than one sense (in this case, adding the sense of touch to the sense of sight) causes your child to be more focused and more likely to remember what she is learning. By placing the letters in alphabetical order, you are providing reinforcement of that order.

Letter Bingo

Purpose: This game encourages your child to associate a sound with the letter of the alphabet that represents that sound, helping your child develop print awareness.

Materials Needed: For this game, you will need to create bingo-type cards with a letter of the alphabet in each of the squares. You do not have to put the letters in alphabetic order in this game, as you are also reinforcing your child's skill in recognizing letters placed randomly. Use a card of no more than six squares when playing with children in the early grades. You can increase the number of squares as your child starts to read and is learning phonics, the alphabet, and that the letters of the alphabet correspond to specific sounds. You will also need tokens or squares of blank paper to cover the letters that correspond to the sounds called. The caller will need a bag with tiles or cards marked with the individual letters.

Number of Players: 4 or more players (1 player will be the caller)

Time: Allow 5 to 10 minutes for each round, depending upon the number of squares on the boards.

How to Play: Give each player a bingo-type card with letters that represent different sounds. The caller (you or your older child until the younger children are more proficient at this skill) pulls a letter from a bag and says the sound made by that letter. The other players must cover the letter that makes that sound. The play continues until one child has covered all the letters on his card. The caller then can uncover the pictures on the winning card, say the name of the letter, and say the name of the sound in order to reinforce the skill.

Modifications for Older Children: Your older child can be the caller. This game provides excellent practice and reinforcement of your older child's skills. Additional practice, even at this level, can help with fluency.

Hints and Variations: Some letters represent more than one sound, so you can allow your child to choose a different letter than the one drawn from the bag if it is appropriate. For example, if the caller pulls the letter *k* and says the sound /k/, a player may cover the letter *c* if she is thinking of the hard sound that the letter *c* has in a word like *cat*.

Make sure the caller hides the letter that is drawn from the bag so that it does not become a visual matching game. However, if your child is having difficulty or if you want to play this with younger children or children having difficulty remembering letter sounds, you can make it a visual matching game and show the letter to the players so they can see if they have a match.

When the caller uncovers the answers and calls out the sound, that provides important opportunities to reinforce the skill. Because many letter/sound combinations are given before the winner of the round is revealed, your child may make mistakes that are not corrected until the end of the game. Peek at your child's board occasionally to make sure she is covering the correct letter.

Skills Developed: Once your child has learned the sounds in a word, he must learn the letter that is associated with each sound in order to be able to read the printed word. One of the first steps in learning to read is recognizing the uppercase and lowercase letters and knowing which sound or sounds each letter makes. (This is often referred to as the ABCs but is not always as easy as ABC!)

Then reading involves knowing that the sequence of letters in a written word is the same as the sequence of sounds in the word when it is spoken. Your child will benefit from practicing the letter names and sounds as often as possible in the early years. Once the letter sounds are automatically recalled, the information will be stored in long-term memory, and he will be able to use his mental energy in blending sounds and recalling words rather than in recalling individual sounds. This will help him read fluently, with speed and accuracy—skills that will aid with comprehension.

Print It

Purpose: This game helps your child associate the sounds of letters and words with the written letters and words.

Materials Needed: This game can be played with a variety of materials. You can use aluminum pans from the supermarket and fill them with sand or salt. You can use the same pans with pudding that has a heavy consistency. You can use sticks, pipe cleaners, or strings coated with wax that you buy in a toy or art supply store. You will also need a bag with tiles that have the letters of the alphabet on them. You can make them from pieces of cardboard or use the tiles from a commercial game. At your option, you can use an egg timer to see who can complete the task the fastest.

Number of Players: 2 to 4

Time: Allow 5 to 10 minutes so you are not rushed and everyone can have fun playing.

How to Play: Each player, in turn, is the caller. The caller pulls a letter tile or card from the bag, keeps it hidden from the other players, and says the letter sound. The other players must "write" the letter in the material you have chosen to use. For example, if you are using sand in an aluminum tray, the players trace the letter in the sand. If you are using pipe cleaners or waxed strings, you will need to provide more time for the players to form the letters. The player who finishes the letter first gets 1 point for that round.

Modifications for Older Children: Playing with the pudding, sand, or waxed strings can be a huge draw in getting your older children to participate in this game. You can make this game more difficult by putting three- and four-letter words in the bag. If you have children of different ages, the caller would say the word, and the younger child would write the beginning sound while the older child would write the whole word.

Hints and Variations: This game can be messy, so you don't want to have too many players. A way to control the mess is to put a smaller amount of the pudding, sand, or salt in a plastic bag that can be closed. Once the bag is closed, the material spreads out, and the players can "write" on the top of the bag and make an impression on the material inside. You may need to experiment with the amount to put in the bag. This way the bags can be saved for future play.

You can eliminate the mess entirely by playing the game at a park with a sandbox or at the beach.

Skills Developed: When learning to read, your child needs to understand that letters represent sounds and that the printed word represents a grouping of those sounds. This skill is print awareness, sometimes called alphabetic awareness. You are reinforcing this skill each time you read to your child and put your finger under the word as you read it. You are showing that the symbols on the page have meaning and correspond to what is read. This skill helps him unlock the code of reading and helps with fluency—accuracy and speed of recall of the letters. It is important for your child to be able to say and write the letters of the alphabet fluently, so his reading and writing will be faster than if he has to try to stop and think of the letter each time he goes to write or read a word.

Words, Words, Words

Helping Your Child Strengthen Reading Skills

s stated in Chapter 1, helping our children strengthen their reading and reading readiness skills is one of the most important ways we can spend time with them. As we help them develop phonemic awareness, their reading improves, and as their reading improves, their phonemic awareness skills grow stronger.

Good reading skills help children develop a strong foundation for learning—a lifelong pursuit for all of us. When they see themselves as learners, they will be better able to succeed in all they do in school and later in life.

The Department of Education report *What Works* states, "Children improve their reading ability by reading a lot. Reading achievement is directly related to the amount of reading children do in school and outside." While working as a school librarian, Penny could easily recognize those children who spent time reading at home. The more they read, the more they enjoyed reading.

Research has shown that being unsuccessful at reading in the early years can have terrible consequences for children's development of self-confidence and their motivation to learn and perform in school. Let's go back to the previous chapter's example of traveling to China or another country where you don't speak the language. You don't really expect to know the language right away, but you have confidence that you can learn it over time—at least enough to get by. Don't you? You do if you did not experience failure when you began the process. You do if you can see the relationships between the words in that language and what you already know, and if someone there is encouraging you and helping you as you learn.

As your child learns, her ability to learn increases. Success breeds success, and enjoyment leads to good memories of the learning process. When something we do is fun, we want to continue doing it. When reading is fun for your child, she will want to continue doing it.

Children do not all learn at the same rate, but there are natural progressions for the skill of reading. We can't keep our children from comparing themselves with the other children in their class, but we can encourage them as they develop their own skills. When we take the time to be with them and make learning fun, we show that we have confidence in them and in their ability to learn and be readers.

The games in this section are exciting and educational. Your children will be having fun and probably won't even realize they are also developing their thinking skills at the same time.

You can begin by helping your child improve her ability to read and to understand what she is reading. You can help her move beyond phonemic awareness through word recognition to fluency— the ability to read quickly, accurately, and with good understanding. You can help her recall specific facts, and more important, you can help her to that next level of reading, the ability to draw conclusions based on what she has read. If your child reads about termites, she will probably read that they are small creatures capable of doing major damage to wooden structures. You want your child to take that information to the next step and understand or assume that you would call an exterminator if you found them in your house. When she reads about dolphins, you want her to remember the specific information she read, but you also want her to begin to understand why environmental groups are working so hard to save these animals.

Schools do, of course, work on comprehension skills and place much emphasis on the "WH" questions: *who, what, when, where, why*. The *who, what, when*, and *where* questions involve memory and the ability to recall, but our children also need to develop the skills to answer the *why* questions in order to analyze and generalize—to apply what they have learned to their own lives.

Your child probably knows the story "Little Red Riding Hood." If so, she can tell you the main characters, the *who* of the book. She can probably tell you *where* Little Red Riding Hood was going, *what* she was wearing, and probably even the time of day. But when you begin asking the *why* questions, many children begin to lose confidence. Why did the wolf choose Red as his victim? (Was he attracted by her cape?)

And this is just a simple fairy tale. What happens when children begin reading more complex material? Will they have the thinking skills to understand more than the basic details? In a relaxed home setting, and with you as a guide, your child will have the time and the encouragement to practice the thinking skills she will need as the work gets more difficult.

We want our children to be readers, and we can encourage them to read. We want them to develop sophisticated thinking skills, and we can encourage them to think. We want them to feel successful, and we can provide opportunities for that success. With the activities in this chapter, we can help them develop their reading and thinking skills, as well as their confidence.

The games in this chapter give your children positive experiences with the written word, with reading, and with books. These games will encourage your child to want to read, and they will help her read creatively and productively, improving her comprehension skills.

The previous chapter focused on phonemic awareness, the skills a child needs to learn the mechanics of reading. In this chapter, the emphasis will be on helping your child think about what she is reading. The games encourage children to detect the main idea. They provide opportunities for comparing and contrasting and for examining cause and effect. The games teach children to classify and interpret information and help them make judgments and predictions. They include opportunities to use books, magazines, and maps to help your child develop solid research and exploration skills. All of this practice improves vocabulary, and best of all, your child will be spending enjoyable time with you.

Although these games help develop reading and verbal skills, we strongly encourage you also to spend at least part of every day reading aloud to your child. A period of reading time set aside each day will help your child develop not only the skills needed for reading success, but also a joy of language that you can share while snuggled in a favorite chair or curled up in bed.

Because children's listening skills are usually more advanced than their reading abilities, when you read to your child, you share information well above her reading level. As she watches you read, place your finger beneath the words as you read them. Watching you, your child learns to associate the spoken word with the written one—an essential skill.

You can make the most of your reading sessions by making them interactive. Most children like to hear the same story read again and again. Instead of just rereading the story, have your child look at the pictures and help you tell the story. Or ask, "What is going to happen on this page?" or "What is going to happen next?" You can have your child repeat phrases as you read them or, if she is beginning to read on her own, take turns reading sentences or phrases, helping as necessary. Once you have finished reading, talk about the story.

In addition to reading with children, you can help strengthen their skills by playing games designed to improve their recall, comprehension, and interpretation. The following games are designed to enhance your read-aloud sessions. Although the skills developed with these games are serious skills, the games are not. These are not classroom activities. Giggling, laughing, and generous applause are encouraged. Have fun!

Funny-Paper Fun

Purpose: This game helps your child develop skills in comprehension, sequencing (putting things in their proper order), and cause and effect.

Materials Needed: You will need comic strips, scissors, and pencils for this game. Use the comics pages of a newspaper, children's magazine, or commercial comic book. Many cartoons are available online, too.

Number of Players: 2 (This game can be played with more players if you have more than 1 child, but playing it in a one-to-one environment gives your child a little undivided attention.)

Time: Allow at least 15 minutes for one round. If you have more time, each player can present more than one comic strip.

How to Play: The object of this game is for players to successfully rearrange scrambled comic strips. Each player chooses a favorite comic strip. Your rebel might choose "Calvin and Hobbes." A sensitivity specialist might choose "Peanuts." Cat lovers would probably choose "Garfield." Each player numbers the back of each panel of the strip in order (1, 2, 3, 4), cuts the strip into panels, and scrambles the pieces. Pencils are best for this activity, as the ink of pens shows through the other side. The players trade strips. Each player arranges the pieces of the other player's strip in correct order. The first to finish unscrambling correctly wins.

Modifications for Older Children: When you are playing with children who know how to read, be sure to select comic strips that have words. Older children will need to sequence the comics based on the written language.

Hints and Variations: When played for more than one round, it is possible to allow a little more variety and creativity. The player who comes up with the correct sequence of the strip could be awarded 5 points, but if your child is able to come up with a story that justifies a different sequence of the strip's pieces, he should be awarded bonus points.

If you are using the newspaper, save the comics for a few days in order to offer more choices.

Let the preschooler (or nonreader) tell you what he thinks is happening in the cartoon and make up a story to go with the pictures. Preschoolers look at events so differently than we do, and their versions often create enjoyable variations. Young children love telling stories, and parents love hearing them. What could be more fun?

Skills Developed: For your child to understand what he reads, he must understand what happens first, second, third, and so on. He has to see how events happen in a logical order and that one event can cause another. This is particularly important in social studies and in reading biographies. When memorizing history facts, your child must know that the Revolutionary War came before the Civil War and after the pilgrims landed at Plymouth Rock. By using comic strips to develop this sequencing skill, your child is able to use his own language to make sense of the events of the story presented in the strip.

The Same Game

Purpose: This game helps your child categorize information and encourages vocabulary development.

Materials Needed: This activity does not involve any materials and is a good one to play in a car or while waiting.

Number of Players: 2 or more (teams of up to 10)

Time: Each round could take 5 minutes or more, depending on the level of difficulty. Save this one for when you have a long stretch of uninterrupted time.

How to Play: In this game, players guess the category that a group of words fits into. One player thinks of a category (for example, sharp things), which she does not reveal, and then names an object that belongs to that category (for example, knife). The other players try to guess the secret category. The original player names additional objects that belong in the same category—razor, then pencil point, and so on—until one of the players can guess the correct category. The player who guesses correctly earns 1 point and thinks of the next category. If no one is able to guess the category (or come close) after the presenter has given at least five examples, the original player wins the point and the right to another turn.

Modifications for Older Children: This game is ideal for older children. Their vocabulary will allow them to come up with many more words that fit into a category. Because older children more readily recognize that objects can belong to more than one category, they can really have fun with this game.

Hints and Variations: This activity might be more difficult for younger children, so rather than making it an individual effort, you might divide the players into teams. With this and other more difficult activities, be sure to give points for sense of humor and a friendly, cooperative manner. Some suggestions for possible categories include color, hot things, cold things, heavy things, silly things. Have fun.

Skills Developed: Children need to understand that words can have more than one meaning. Successful education requires flexible thinking, and the ability to do well on standardized tests depends on it. Your child must be aware that many words have more than one meaning and can fit into more than one category. The word *light* can refer to weight, the opposite of dark, or fewer calories or reduced fat. When children play with words in this way, they develop the ability to recognize multiple meanings, and they broaden their vocabulary at the same time.

Predictions

Purpose: This game encourages your child to look for patterns in reading material and to be a keen observer of the world. It also helps develop study skills.

Materials Needed: No materials are needed, but this game should be played in a place of activity or changing environment, such as in a car, restaurant, or other public place.

Number of Players: 2 to a carful

Time: Each turn can take 5 minutes or more, so Predictions is good for a long car trip.

How to Play: The object of the game is for players to predict what will happen next. Each player, in turn, poses a question relevant to the environment. For example, in a car, he might ask how many blue cars will pass before a yellow one does. In a restaurant, your child might ask how quickly your water glasses will be refilled after you empty them. All players make their predictions and then watch to see what actually happens. The player who comes closest to the actual result is the winner.

Modifications for Older Children: This game is fun for all ages. Older children, who have longer attention spans and better memories, can play this game over a series of days. They can make predictions about things that are going to happen days away, rather than minutes away.

Hints and Variations: To make the play faster and more fun, all players can pose their questions at the same time, so they are waiting and watching for more than one event. Other examples of possible questions are: "Who will be taken next at the doctor's office?" "Which car will try to change lanes first in a traffic jam?" "Which table will receive its food first?"

The one Cheryl's boys liked best was, "How soon will Dad lose his temper when the driver in front of him is going too slowly?"

Skills Developed: The ability to sense cause and effect and to anticipate consequences is important for higher levels of reading comprehension. To be an active reader, your child will need to question what he reads and make predictions about the events before he finishes the material. He needs to think about what he is reading and see if it makes sense. When children question and anticipate as they read, they strengthen their comprehension skills.

 Picka

Purpose: While improving her reading vocabulary, your child improves her powers of observation and develops categorization skills with this game.

Materials Needed: No specific materials are needed. This game can be played at home, in the car, or while waiting in a restaurant or for an office appointment. It provides a constructive use of time that might otherwise be wasted in boredom.

Number of Players: 2 to 6

Time: Each turn takes under 5 minutes, so you can play for as long or as short a time as you have available.

How to Play: The object of the game is to be the last person to provide a word that fits into a particular category. One player chooses a category and tells it to the other players. For example, a category could be round, yellow, or wooden. Then each player, including the one who chose the category, names something she sees that fits into the category. Choices in the round category might be: table, coins, plates, eyes. The winner is the last person who can name something to fit into the category.

The next person chooses another category, and play continues until the time you've allowed for the game is over, or until dinner arrives.

Modifications for Older Children: When playing with older children, you could use more abstract ideas for categories, such as boring (a yawn, unappetizing food, conversation); clinging (clothes, drapes, people); empty (glass, mind, hunger).

Hints and Variations: The complexity of the categories needs to be tailored to the ages of the children. Do not limit creativity in the choice of a category, as that is a major component of the game. When playing in public places, you can teach your child the concept of tact. The waitress should not be included in the round or old category if she can hear the answers! If your child is stuck, feel free to help him think of categories by providing clues: "What about a color?" "What about a shape?"

As this game is the reverse of the Same Game, described earlier in this chapter, you might want to use these two games interchangeably. In the Same Game, your child takes specific clues and finds their broad category. In Picka, she tries to find words that fit into a known category.

Skills Developed: Your child needs to understand similarities and differences in concrete items as well as abstract ideas. A table and a chair are both pieces of furniture, but they have different uses. Love and hate are both emotions, but they have very different expressions. She needs to be able to identify words by their relationship to other words and to be able to group words into categories.

This game requires each player to choose a category for her turn and to provide words that are examples of that category. She might have to use her imagination and powers of persuasion to prove a word she chooses belongs in a particular category. (If she can support the idea that Santa Claus fits into the round category, let her do so.) Your child will develop planning strategies when selecting a category. With practice, she will learn to choose a broad category, such as sports, rather than a very limited category, such as words that rhyme with *oranges*.

Location, Please

Purpose: This game gives your child a better sense of the world and his place in it, and it helps him improve his map-reading skills.

Materials Needed: For this game, you will need a map, an atlas, or a globe. For younger children, you should begin with a large map of one state and progress to maps of countries and continents as the child gains proficiency in map skills. (If you play as suggested in Hints and Variations, you will need a game board and dice.)

Number of Players: 2 to 6

Time: Each round will take from 5 to 10 minutes. Play as many rounds as you have time for.

How to Play: The object of this game is to be the first one to discover a secret location on a map. Taking turns, each player chooses a secret place on a map of your state, the United States, or the world. The secret location can be a mountain, a river, or a city. The secret location can be as precise as Central Park on a map of New York

City or as general as the Atlantic Ocean on a globe. The other players ask yes/no questions to obtain information about the location. For example, using the map of the United States, the secret location might be Boston. Possible questions would include "Are you in a city?" "Are you in New England?" and "Are you in Massachusetts?" The first player to guess the correct location gets a point. The player with the most points at the end of the available time wins.

Modifications for Older Children: When playing with older children, you can use world maps. As children get more knowledgeable with their geography skills, they will begin to select more exotic locations as their secret spot. They may choose the Seychelles or Tasmania, for example.

Hints and Variations: It's also fun to play this game with a game board. The first player to guess the correct location rolls the dice and moves around the board. If you construct your own game board, why not make a city in the home spot? When children create their own game board, they can decorate it with rivers, mountains, and oceans to make the board more interesting. They might also include penalty squares and bonus squares—such as lose a turn or move 2 extra spaces. Many elementary school children do not fully understand the meaning of state, city, and country. You can use this activity to help them come to a better understanding of these terms.

Cheryl has even played using a map of her town, which helped her son get to his friend's house on his bike.

Skills Developed: Reading is not limited to words. A child also needs to be able to obtain information from charts, graphs, and maps. Throughout school, he will be exposed to maps in social studies and in geography. He will need to be able to locate cities, rivers, and countries and to understand their relationships to each other. Maps are an important source of information about our ever-changing world. This activity provides a fun way to work with a map and will encourage your child to see the location of an area within the framework of a larger geographical sphere. A better understanding of world geography fosters a clearer understanding of world events and how they affect us. When teaching research skills in the library, Penny was often surprised at how little experience her students had in this area.

ogus

Purpose: This game helps your child become more familiar with using a dictionary and makes her more aware of the multiple meanings of words.

Materials Needed: For this game, you will need a dictionary. Be sure to use a dictionary that is appropriate to the reading level of your child. Many dictionaries are available in picture versions. Online dictionaries are also available. You will also need a game board, markers, and dice. You can use a commercial game board from another game or create your own. You could also use the outside squares of a checkerboard.

Number of Players: 2 or more players and an adult supervisor

Time: Allow at least 30 minutes to complete your way around the game board.

How to Play: The object of the game is to guess the correct meaning of a word when the actual meaning and a fabricated meaning are given. Players roll a die and the one who rolls the highest number goes first. Play rotates.

The first player chooses a word from the dictionary and presents both the actual definition and a definition she has invented. For example, the word chosen might be *bogus*. The actual definition might be *not genuine*. A fabricated definition might be *a tropical moss*. A more advanced player might use a word such as *terminate* as the chosen word.

The next player must guess the correct definition. If the guess is correct, she rolls the die and moves the number of spaces indicated. If she is incorrect, the player who presented the definition rolls and moves. The first to circle the board wins.

Modifications for Older Children: This game is suitable for all ages. Because skill development can be so different among age groups, this game is best played when the players are close to the same age. Older players, of course, will use more difficult words.

Hints and Variations: As mentioned above, this game works better if the players are close in age and if you act as helper to all of them. It would be difficult for them to stump you with a bogus definition. If you create your own game board, you can include bonus squares such as roll again or penalty squares such as move back 2 spaces to add more of the element of chance to the game. These bonus and penalty squares could help your younger child move around the board quicker.

Skills Developed: Your child will need to be able to use a dictionary throughout her years in school. After she graduates, many jobs, including teaching, secretarial positions, writing, and editorial work, require the continued use of a dictionary. The dictionary is usually the first reference children use. By helping develop your child's ability to use one, you will be helping her build the skills she will need later in order to use the encyclopedia and more advanced reference materials.

In her effort to come up with obscure words to present, she will broaden her own vocabulary. Young children enjoy making up meanings for words, and this will provide them with a creative outlet. Remind your child that it is important to keep a straight face when giving a bogus answer.

ind It

Purpose: This game is designed to give your child practice in using reference books to find information and will make him aware of the kinds of reference materials available.

Materials Needed: You will need a dictionary, encyclopedia, thesaurus, or atlas and a timer.

Number of Players: 2 to 4

Time: Each turn might take 5 to 10 minutes, depending on the reference book used. Finding information in an encyclopedia may take longer than finding it in a dictionary.

How to Play: The object of the game is to locate the answer to a specific question by finding the answer in a dictionary, encyclopedia, thesaurus, atlas, or other reference. Each player, in turn, asks a question that can only be answered by finding information in a reference book. If your child has difficulty formulating a question, let him skim through the reference book for ideas. The next player is given a time limit in which to find the answer. Allow 5 minutes for questions that use a dictionary or thesaurus and 10 minutes for questions that need an encyclopedia or atlas. If he is able to find the answer, he wins that round. If he cannot locate the information, the player who asked the question must be able to show the answer in the reference book, and he is the winner. Older children should be expected to find answers to specific questions, such as, "How many people live in our state?" Penny often played this game with her students in the library to give them practice using the reference section. Preschoolers might be asked to find the page with the information about airplanes in a picture dictionary.

Modifications for Older Children: Many older children love sports and enjoy finding sports trivia. Others enjoy finding out about unusual information. The *Guinness Book of World Records* and sports almanacs can be especially appealing to older players.

Hints and Variations: Many excellent reference books are now available in paperback, and many others are available at the library. If you can't check these books out of your library, you could play the game in the children's room. For your younger children, look for books that contain mostly pictures. If children of different ages and ability levels are playing, use different sets of reference books, and make sure you oversee the questions asked to make sure your younger child has a chance to find the answer. You could form teams with the children, or 2 children could team up against you. To make the game go faster, all players can pose questions at the same time, and the person to find each answer first is the winner.

Skills Developed: Research skills can help us all find the answers to questions. Many children are not even aware of reference materials and do not realize they are able to find the information they need. Your child needs to learn that no one is expected to know everything. The ability to use these resources will help him know when, how, and where to seek help. It will also help him become more of an independent learner and will allow him to broaden his knowledge.

Details

Purpose: This game encourages your child to listen carefully and to pay attention to details.

Materials Needed: You will need books or magazine articles for this game. Have a variety available, so your child will be able to choose. Make sure the books or articles are about subjects she enjoys or ones you would like her to enjoy, but let her choose.

Number of Players: 2 to 3 (best played with 2)

Time: You should allow at least 15 minute to get the full enjoyment of this game. That will give you and your child time for one turn each. If you can play longer, you will be able to have more than one turn.

How to Play: The object of the game is to remember as many details as possible based on the information that is presented. Have your child choose the book to be read. You read a passage from the book that contains a complete idea and ask your child how many details she can restate from what was read. She will receive 1 point for each detail remembered. Next, your child will tell a story and ask you for details. She then decides if you answered correctly and how many points you earned. The winner is the player with the most points at the end of all turns.

Modifications for Older Children: Once your child is old enough to read on her own, let her read a section from her school texts when it is her turn to present. This is a fun way to reinforce material your child is learning in school and provides you with an opportunity to hear her read.

Hints and Variations: This might be a good way to get your child to tell you about her day in school. We all are too familiar with the "Nothing" response when we ask our child what happened during the school day. When she is challenging you to remember details, her stories must become more elaborate.

While Cheryl was playing this game with her son, she finally discovered why he came home each day with holes in the knees of his jeans. Instead of simply saying, "I fell," he gave her a detailed description of the daily cannonball games (a form of dodgeball) played at recess.

If you are playing with more than 1 child, you can give each child a turn to choose the book and answer the questions. If there is a big age difference between the children, you can set a rule ahead of time that you might be giving hints to help the younger child remember details. Be as lenient as possible in your scoring. You want to make sure your child will want to play again.

Skills Developed: The most important reading activity a parent can do with a child, no matter what age, is to read aloud to her. This can expose her to materials well above her actual reading level. Most children's listening comprehension is more developed than their reading comprehension. In addition to providing a quiet time for interaction, this activity gives your child some control by allowing her to choose the book herself. This activity can be used with all children, no matter what their reading ability, since you will be doing all of the reading.

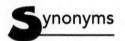 **S**ynonyms

Purpose: This game helps your child understand how to use a thesaurus and how to practice using words with similar meanings.

Materials Needed: You will need a thesaurus for this game. If you cannot find an appropriate thesaurus, use a child's dictionary. The definitions are usually short and more like synonyms than in a regular dictionary. Public libraries usually have circulation copies of these. You will also need a game board. Take one from any commercial game, or construct your own with cardboard and markers.

Number of Players: The more, the merrier

Time: Allow 20 minutes or more.

How to Play: Explain to your child that synonyms are words that have the same or similar meanings. You can give examples to explain how words mean the same thing: big/large, tiny/small, bucket/pail. The object of the game is to give as many words as possible that mean the same thing as the clue word. When playing with young children, you choose a word from the thesaurus and ask for a synonym. Each player gives one synonym in turn and moves his marker 1 space on the game board until the ideas are exhausted. For example, if the clue word is *sport*, synonyms would be *game, hobby, contest,* *fun, play*. Then a new word is chosen, and the procedure is repeated. The last to give a correct guess gets a bonus move and goes first in the next round. The first player to make a complete circle of the board is the winner.

Modifications for Older Children: Older children can play for points. Play rotates. Each player, in turn, chooses a word from the thesaurus. All players, including the one who chose the word, list as many synonyms as they can think of on a piece of paper. Players read their lists aloud and cross off any words that were listed by any other player. Score 1 point for each correct word that no one else has chosen. The player with the most points at the end of the allotted time is the winner. For each round, allow 3 to 5 minutes to complete the lists.

Hints and Variations: This game requires abstract thinking and might not be appropriate for the very young child. It is a good game to play with your child and his friends, as it works better with more players. The use of a game board makes it more like a commercial game, and that appeals to many children.

Skills Developed: The ability to find an answer from the appropriate source is often as important as knowing the answer. Your child needs to be comfortable using a thesaurus (some are available online), because it is a skill he will use throughout his school years. As he begins to do more creative writing, he will need to be able to find words to give the proper meaning to what he writes. When he knows that the words are available to him in a book or online, creative writing becomes an easier task. This game develops reading skills that can be put to use when writing.

 **Word Hunt**

Purpose: This game will help your child develop her skills in categorization.

Materials Needed: Children's magazines. *Weekly Reader* is a good choice, and most schools allow children to bring them home. Colored pencils or pens are optional.

Number of Players: 2 to 4

Time: Each round should take approximately 10 minutes.

How to Play: The object of the game is to find all the nouns, verbs, or adjectives and adverbs within a reading selection. Each player chooses an article from a children's magazine. If you are participating, use a regular magazine or a newspaper for your selection. Each player chooses a particular category. Since your child may not know the terms *noun, verb, adjective,* and *adverb,* use category designations she will understand. If you are searching for nouns, make the category *people, places, and things.* If you are searching for verbs, call the category *action words.* When searching for adjectives or adverbs, the category might be called *words that describe.*

Once the category is determined, each player searches her article and circles all the words that fit into that category. An example of words in the people, places, and things category in a sentence about Coca-Cola would be: *Coca-Cola* is a *drink* that has become unusually popular in *America* and throughout the *world.* Players then read their words aloud. Whoever circles all the correct words within the time limit wins.

To even the odds, you might have a shorter time limit to read your own passage, since your skimming skills are probably faster than your child's!

Modifications for Older Children: Older children can play this game alongside younger children. They simply use more difficult reading materials for the game. They could also use homework assignments, getting some fun out of a task they might not have enjoyed. (If they can't write in the books, you can use transparent tape that is designed to come off easily. You can get this in paper supply stores.) Your older child should understand what nouns, verbs, and adjectives are.

Hints and Variations: If you use a different-colored pen for each specific category, you can then use the same article more than one time.

Before beginning the activity, you might need to help your child read through the article to help her understand what she is reading. To play with a preschooler, use comic strips, and have the child identify pictures that fit into the categories. In that case, you might want to call the categories *people, things, colors,* and *what people are doing.*

Skills Developed: The ability to skim and locate a particular word or concept is an important study skill that is used throughout school and into adult life. Many jobs, including those in education, business, and journalism, require the ability to skim in order to retrieve information in the shortest possible time.

Since your child will be expected to label words as either nouns (people, places, or things), verbs (action words), or adjectives and adverbs (describing words), she will become more aware of the multiple uses of some words. The word *move* might be a noun when it is the move from one house to another, or it might be a verb when you move your checker in a checkers game.

Your child can also use this exercise to increase her vocabulary, because the words you have identified in your reading passage may be unfamiliar to her.

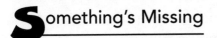

Something's Missing

Purpose: This game requires your child to draw on what he has learned in the past about a specific topic as he reads new material.

Materials Needed: To play, you will need children's magazines (not borrowed), paper and pencils, and a laundry marker or felt-tipped marker.

Number of Players: 2 players or 2 teams of players

Time: Completing the game takes at least 30 minutes.

How to Play: The object of the game is to guess the words that are missing from a sentence by using the context of the sentence for clues. Each player chooses a sentence from a different children's magazine article and copies two or three words from the sentence on a piece of paper, which he keeps hidden. Players then use a marker to eliminate those words from the text. Each player announces the subject of his article and then trades his sentence for the other player's or other team's sentence. Each player examines the sentence and tries to figure out the missing words, based on what he knows about the subject. For example, a sentence from an article about food might be, "Plants, animals, and people must have food in order to grow and to keep healthy." The words *animals*, *food*, and *healthy* might be marked out, and the other player would have to try to guess what they are. Don't take out all important words, because there would be no context left to help with guesses. Each player or team gets 1 point for each correct guess, and the player or team with the most points wins.

Modifications for Older Children: Have your older child copy a sentence or two from his homework assignment or from one of his textbooks. He can then eliminate several words and have you try to guess what they are. When it is your turn, you can copy information from his books, eliminate some words, and have him try to figure out what is missing. This will provide you with an opportunity to see how his reading comprehension is developing.

Hints and Variations: If a particular task appears to be confusing for your child, make sure you take the first turn. The child will learn how to use the context of the sentence by watching the way you do it. You can orally go through the steps you are taking, so the child will have some idea of how to approach the task. You would read the sentence aloud, saying the word *blank* at each missing word, and play around with a few words to see if any of them make sense in that place. If you are playing with a preschooler, you will want to team up with the child and let him help you fill in the blanks with information you provide orally.

A variation of this game would allow you to give points for answers other than the correct ones if the child uses the correct type of word (noun, verb) and creates a sentence with a high degree of originality and humor (points for the creative process).

If they can't write in the magazines, you can use transparent tape or Post-it notes that are designed to come off easily. Use the tape to put a piece of paper over the word you want to leave out. You can get the tape in paper supply stores.

Skills Developed: Much of what your child learns in school is built upon previous learning. The child's common question, "Why do I need to know that?" is often answered with reference to future courses of study, but the future seems so far away that the answer has little meaning for him. He needs to understand that all learning, no matter how trivial it appears, is important in building a framework for future exploration. He needs to see that the future can be as close as tomorrow or five minutes from now, and that it will be necessary for him to apply what he has learned to new situations. What we read has meaning to us because of things we have already learned. When a child reads that a sailor is lost at sea, he knows the sailor is surrounded by water but will have nothing to drink. The child has previously learned that the ocean contains salt water and humans cannot drink it.

To guess the missing words in this activity, your child will need to draw on information he has already learned about the subject presented. This task needs to be approached in a methodical and orderly fashion, so Something's Missing encourages logical as well as abstract and creative thinking.

ot It!

Purpose: This game helps your child learn how to skim through written material to find important information.

Materials Needed: You will need children's magazines for this game. This is a good way for you to encourage your child to read all of those magazines you subscribe to for her but she never seems to open.

Number of Players: 2 to 4

Time: Allow at least 30 minutes for this game, to allow time for several rounds.

How to Play: The object of this game is to find specific information from an article by skimming. Each participant chooses the article she will read from a children's magazine. The articles used by the players should be of approximately the same length. At the beginning of each round, one player announces whether the players will be expected to find who or what the article is about, where it took place, or when it happened. Each player takes a turn choosing the category. The winner is the first to find the answer to the question in her article and to call out "Got it!" In case of a tie, bonus points could be awarded for answers to a "Why did it happen?" or "How did it happen?" question.

If you are playing with a preschooler, you might read the passage to your child and have her answer the questions. Although this will not develop skimming skills, it will develop listening skills and vocabulary. You can use the same article for more than one round of this game, as the information you will be seeking will be different each time.

Modifications for Older Children: Older children can play this game along with younger children, as long as their reading material is age appropriate.

Hints and Variations: Many articles do not provide all the information players might call for, and expectations will need to be adjusted accordingly. You could also play this game with your child using her homework assignment while you use a magazine you have not had time to read. Use any opportunity to incorporate homework in a relaxed atmosphere. Younger children may choose a favorite picture book. Even if they cannot actually read the story, they would be able to find pictures of the *who, what,* or *where* of the story. For example, your child might look at the story "The Three Little Pigs." He will be able to find the who (the pigs), the what (the bricks, the straw, and sticks), and the where (at the pig's house). You may have to demonstrate a time or two, but he will quickly catch on.

Skills Developed: Skimming skills are important when studying for exams or quizzes, working on reports, and taking standardized tests. Even as adults, when we need to be able to get information fast, we skim an article or recipe for the main points or ingredients. Your child needs to learn that there is more than one way to get information from books and that it is appropriate to take this shortcut in some situations.

Do You Know?

Purpose: This game requires your child to draw conclusions from information he has learned at school or at home and helps improve his vocabulary.

Materials Needed: You will need newspapers or magazines (may be borrowed), pencils and paper, and a dictionary.

Number of Players: Best with 2 or more children plus you as the moderator and helper (It would be difficult for your child to find vocabulary you do not know.)

Time: Allow 15 minutes for each round.

How to Play: The object of this game is to be able to guess the meaning of words given by another player. Using separate newspaper or magazine articles, players choose two to three words that the other players may not know about a particular topic. The players each write their words on a slip of paper. Each player, in turn, presents aloud the topic of his article and his words. The other players, in turn, get a chance to define each word until someone is successful or until they all give up. The presenting player gets 1 point for each word that cannot be defined by the other players. The players providing the definitions receive 1 point for each word that is correctly defined. The player with the most points at the end of the round is the winner.

Weekend newspapers often include a special section for children. These are terrific for this game. A recent example included an article about a spy museum. The words *shredder*, *bug*, and *ultimate* were new to Penny's grandchildren.

Modifications for Older Children: Older children would play this game with more challenging reading materials. This is a great way to get them to start reading the newspaper and learning about current events.

Hints and Variations: You may need a dictionary to verify definitions in case of a dispute. Disputes are very helpful in games like these, because they encourage each child to defend his choices by using many different language skills to persuade and convince. You might be cultivating a debater or a future politician.

When Penny played this game with her children, they enjoyed stumping her with their knowledge of sports terms.

An interesting variation might be for each player to tell the other players the words to be defined but not the article topic. The other players not only have to define the words, but also must guess the topic of the article.

Skills Developed: Your child needs to be aware of the vocabulary that is specific to a particular topic, so he can more fully understand the topic. When he reads about cowboys, it helps if he is familiar with words such as *lariat, herds,* and *branding.* This game forces him to look at the context and vocabulary of an article and try to guess the meaning of a word from the information he knows about a subject. He must understand that words create a picture of a complete idea. He will be choosing words for his opponents that he hopes they will not know. In doing so, he will be stretching his vocabulary. When it is his turn to give meanings for his opponent's words, he will have to clearly state his definitions. The way he uses language to form a complete thought will be important here.

Categories

Purpose: This game helps your child with her skills in skimming and categorizing and provides practice in charting information.

Materials Needed: You will need children's magazines, newspaper, paper, and pencils.

Number of Players: 2 to 4

Time: Allow 30 minutes for this game.

How to Play: The object of the game is to locate words to fill the category spaces on a chart. Each player enters three agreed-upon category topics at the top of her page, chooses a four- to six-letter name or word found in a magazine article, and writes the letters of the word down the side of her page. For example:

	Places	Actions	Describing Words
S			
H			
A			
R			
K			

Other categories you could use at the top of the page are songs, colors, food, animals, or anything else agreed upon by the players.

Each player must fill in the columns on her chart with words that begin with the letter at the left side and fit the category. Besides the word written down the left side, all the words entered in the chart for each category must come from her chosen magazine article. It may not be possible to fill all the spaces. For example, in an article about baseball, players might find the following words:

	People	Places	Things
P		park	popcorn
E	Epstein		
D	Damon	dugout	
R			
O	outfielder		

Award 1 point for each word placed correctly in a given time limit. The player with the most points wins.

You will want to decide how much time to allow for each round, depending on how successful the players are. If you feel your child wants to spend more time on each round, encourage her to do so.

Modifications for Older Children: Older children enjoy playing this game when they can read the sports or entertainment pages of the newspaper. Once again, homework assignments could be used for this game as well, giving your child an opportunity to break down the reading assignment into categories, helping to reinforce learning.

Hints and Variations: If you are playing alone with a child, you could use a more difficult magazine to complete your portion. Keep in mind that adults can write much more quickly than children, so take your time. If you are playing with a preschooler, you will want to form teams. You can read the word for the child and ask her to place it in the proper category.

You can also play this game by using words at random to fill in the spaces. This variation does not involve reading, but it does involve practice in grouping words by category and understanding how charts are created.

Skills Developed: Getting information by reading charts is an important skill. Your child will have a better idea of how to read charts if she has the opportunity to create her own. By providing examples of items that fit into a particular category, she'll gain practice in grouping words by category. The more she understands about particular words or ideas, the more meaning she will be able to get from what she reads.

pposites

Purpose: This game helps your child understand the language of opposites and develops the imagination.

Materials Needed: No materials are needed, but this game needs to be played in a place with a lot of activity. It provides a fun way to divert young children during a long wait in a restaurant or on a long car ride, and creates a positive interaction in a situation that could easily be negative.

Number of Players: 2 to 4

Time: Allow 5 minutes for each round.

How to Play: The object of the game is to find as many objects as possible that can be described by a given set of opposites. Each player takes a turn choosing two opposing categories: short/tall, round/square, fast/slow, and the like. Taking turns, each player finds and names a type of object or person that could fit both categories. For example, if the categories are short/tall, a waitress could be short or tall, a glass could be short or tall, and a plant could be short or tall. The last person to find something to fit both of the opposing categories is the winner of that round. A new set of opposites is chosen, and the game is repeated.

Modifications for Older Children: This game is appropriate for all ages. Older children may choose more difficult words like *scrawny* and *humongous*.

Hints and Variations: This game might be difficult for preschoolers, and parents might want to play in teams with them. You might need to help with the idea of opposites by supplying the first example and letting your child give its opposite. For example, you might say a plant could be tall and allow him to say that a plant could be short. Give praise for choosing unusual and challenging opposite categories—dull/shiny, smooth/rough—as that involves as much creative thinking as coming up with the answers.

Skills Developed: Your child will develop a better understanding of the concept of opposites as he begins to understand that a single object can be described with contrasting words. While playing this game, your child will choose an opposite category, for example, empty/full. Then he will search for an item that could be described in the abstract using either of the terms. If he finds a glass in the room, he knows that a glass might be either empty or full. A wastebasket can be full, and it can be empty. And the same goes for a cardboard box or a bookshelf. He will use his imagination as he searches for objects and tries to visualize both opposite characteristics.

ecall

Purpose: This game helps your child improve her visual memory skills and develops her ability to read for detail.

Materials Needed: You will need a book. Try to use books that are a part of your child's homework.

Number of Players: 2 to 4

Time: Allow at least 30 minutes for this game, since everyone will have to read the same passage.

How to Play: The object of the game is to remember as many details as possible about a passage read silently from a book. Choose a paragraph in a book that can be read by all the players. Together, the players read the paragraph silently, and then turn over the page. The players, in turn, tell one detail they remember about the paragraph. Play continues around the circle until the players run out of details. The last player to remember a detail that has not been previously described is the winner. Since the first player has an advantage, rotate the first turn for each round. This game is similar to Details but focuses on actual reading and memory skills rather than listening skills.

If none of the players can read, you can use a picture with a great deal of action. The players will be allowed the same amount of time to look at the picture before you turn it over. Players, in turn, will tell what they remember about the picture. The last player to remember a new detail wins.

Modifications for Older Children: Older children can select magazine articles they find appealing—an article from a sports magazine, fashion magazine, or automotive magazine might interest older children. Older children might also be expected to read more than one paragraph for a round of play. This will provide more practice in reading and be more taxing on their memory skills, since the selection will contain more information.

Hints and Variations: Use books your child has brought home from school. This is a good way to help her to do her homework and gives her an incentive to remember what she has read.

You will have an easier time reading the passage and remembering the details, which may present a competition problem. One way to remedy this is for you to read the paragraph aloud to everyone, and then the players can tell the details. While this method of play will not improve visual memory skills, it will improve listening skills. If your child has a reading difficulty and the teacher has suggested that you read her homework with her, this is a good way to help her complete it in a reasonable amount of time.

Skills Developed: The ability to remember the details of what she reads is crucial to your child's understanding of a passage. To recall the facts of a paragraph, your child must focus on the details of the written material and fit them together into a complete idea. She can develop her memory with practice, and this game encourages that practice by presenting both a challenge and a reward. She will be learning how to concentrate and will improve her attention span.

Passing most tests—both teacher-made and standardized—requires this ability. As adults, we are constantly expected to remember the details of what we read, both for paid jobs (newscaster, stockbroker, letter carrier) and for our work inside the home (family chef, children's nurse, in-house plumber).

Password

Purpose: This game exposes your child to rich vocabulary and encourages him to connect words with their meanings.

Materials Needed: You will need children's magazines, schoolbooks, or resource books (such as an encyclopedia or a thesaurus), pencils, and index cards or small pieces of paper.

Number of Players: At least 2 (better with 3 or more)

Time: Allow 10 to 15 minutes for each round.

How to Play: One player, the presenter, chooses a word from a magazine, book, dictionary, or other reference source and copies the word, secretly, on a piece of paper. The presenter then gives word clues to all the other players, who try to guess the secret word. For example, for the secret word *airplane*, the clues might be *fly*, *machine*, *pilot*. The presenting player would say "fly" and allow the others to shout out their guesses for the secret word. If no one gets the correct word, the presenter says "machine." Play continues with the presenter giving clues and the others making guesses until the secret word is discovered. If no one can guess the word, the presenter wins that round. At the end of each round, a different player becomes the next presenter.

Modifications for Older Children: No modifications are really needed. Older players will be more familiar with synonyms and will probably have no trouble coming up with like terms. For example, an older child might choose *dirigible* as his secret word. *Blimp*, *airship*, and *Hindenburg* might be the clues.

Hints and Variations: Preschool children can play this game in teams. They would not be able to write the words, but they could choose words from a picture book for someone else to write down. Allow the child to give clues of more than one or two words if that is the only way he can do so successfully. You will be aiming for the child to use related terms, but he might not be ready to function at that level.

This game can be played in a car or restaurant without the benefit of pencil and paper. In this case, everyone will have to trust each other not to change the chosen word midway through the round.

If only 2 people are playing, set a timer. The person to guess the secret word of the other player in the shortest amount of time is the winner.

Skills Developed: When a child is stimulated to improve his vocabulary, his interest in reading is also stimulated. When he is more successful in obtaining the meaning from what he reads, he is more eager to take risks in his learning by trying to read more advanced material. In this game, he must choose a secret word that the other players are to identify. Because he provides clues to help the other players guess his word, he will need to be aware of synonyms of the words he chooses.

Standardized tests throughout elementary and high school call for a child to understand synonyms and multiple meanings for words. This skill will also help in doing crossword puzzles, since most clues given are synonyms of the word needed to fill in the puzzle.

Which Sentence?

Purpose: This game encourages imaginative thinking and an understanding of how ideas go together to form sentences.

Materials Needed: You will need a book (perhaps a schoolbook), pencils, and paper.

Number of Players: 4 to 6

Time: Allow 15 minutes for each round.

How to Play: The object of this game is to create a sentence that other players will choose as the one having come from a book. Each presenter, in turn, chooses any sentence from a book and tells the other players the first letter of each word in that sentence. The other players create sentences using the beginning letters in the order given, write their sentences on a piece of paper, and hand the paper to the presenter. The presenter copies the actual sentence on a piece of paper. For example, the sentence chosen from the book for E, C, H, F, W could be *Every car has four wheels*. Created sentences might include *Each cat has five wives* and *Eating candy helps fifty ways*.

Then the presenter reads all the sentences aloud, in random order, to the other players, and each player guesses which sentence she thinks is the original. Players signal their guess by holding their hand up for the one they choose when it is read the second time. A player receives 1 point for guessing the correct sentence and another for having someone choose her sentence. The player with the most points wins.

Modifications for Older Children: Older players could create longer sentences. This will give them an opportunity to make other players laugh, and they have the ability to use more creative language. Cheryl's students particularly enjoyed this game, since it gave them a chance to rewrite history. The sentence *Benjamin Franklin was a great American writer* was changed to *Benjamin Franklin wanted a giant African watermelon* and *Benjamin Franklin wore a green angora waistcoat*. Sometimes we just laugh and forget about points.

Hints and Variations: This game is better with 4 or more players. So bring in the neighbors! Why not invite your child's friends over on a rainy afternoon?

To play this game alone with your child, you can take a turn giving the first letters of the words in a chosen sentence. The other player must tell what she thinks the sentence is, based on the context of the book from which the sentence came. A point is awarded for each word that is the same as the one in the original sentence. The player with the most points at the end of the allotted time is the winner.

Skills Developed: This game helps your child develop reading and writing skills. When she is the presenter, she must choose a sentence to read from a book and present each word by only its beginning letter. When she is the player, she must formulate complete sentences using words that begin with specific letters. She will develop a better understanding of how reading and writing are related as she sees that the words in the book are just someone else's ideas written down. The process of playing will take some of the mystery and uncertainty out of both of these skills. She will be able to use her own creativity to try to stump players who might be better readers.

Yellow Pages

Purpose: This game reinforces research skills and helps older children read for detail. It is not appropriate for young children.

Materials Needed: To play, you need a kitchen timer and the yellow pages of a phone book. Borrow extra yellow pages from friends, since this game is enhanced when everyone has a copy to work with.

Number of Players: 2 or more

Time: Allow 5 minutes per round.

How to Play: The object of the game is to locate specific information in the yellow pages of a phone book. One player asks for information that the other player must find in the yellow pages. Tasks might include finding a service station that will tow and finding a pizza restaurant that delivers. The next player must then locate the information in the phone book and show the information she found. Use the timer to see how long it takes for the player to find the entry. That player then asks a question, and the other player is timed. The one who finds the entry in the shortest amount of time is the winner. If the time factor creates an unfair advantage for one player, play this game just for the fun of it without keeping score.

Hints and Variations: Do not be concerned if the request is not worded exactly the same as the category found in the phone book. If asked to find a gas station that tows, your child will have to use some additional skills involving cross-referencing to find the right word for the entry. It might be a good idea to go over some of the categories in the Yellow Pages before playing because few school-aged children are in the habit of using any part of the phone book, much less the yellow pages. If you are playing with more than 2 players, each player presents her request to the other players, and the one who finds her answer first is the winner. (For this variation, you will, of course, need a yellow pages for each player.)

Skills Developed: As your child gets into middle school and high school, she will be expected to do more and more research. All of those alphabetical skills she learns in elementary school will later have to be used for locating information quickly in reference books. She will also be expected to pick out the important information from materials provided. The more familiar she is with this process, the more comfortable she will be when she needs to find information quickly to present in class or to use in a project. The process of locating information is a skill that can be taught.

Trivia

Purpose: This game, for older children, encourages the use of reference materials and provides practice in skimming skills. It is too difficult for younger children.

Materials Needed: You will need any kind of almanac, a game board, markers, and a timer.

Number of Players: 2 or more

Time: Allow 15 to 30 minutes for each round.

How to Play: The object of the game is to locate specific information in an almanac. One player browses in the almanac, finding bits of information he thinks the other players will not know. He asks a question about that information. For example, "What is the capital of Georgia?" "What is the state flower of Arkansas?" or "Who won the World Series in 1970?" If the other player can guess the answer correctly, he can move 2 spaces on the game board. If he does not know the answer, he must look it up in the almanac. If he finds the information in under 2 minutes, he moves along 1 space. If he cannot find the answer in the allotted time, the player who presented the question gets to move 1 space. The player to circle the board first is the winner.

Hints and Variations: You might want to adjust the amount of time allowed to find the answer. If your child is not able to find answers in 2 minutes, adjust the time accordingly. Don't discourage him from reading because it takes too long. If your child finds the answers in well under 2 minutes, adjust the limit to 1 minute.

Trivia games are so popular that this game will appeal to your older child because it will increase his store of trivial information. He will be able to stun his friends when he plays trivia-related games.

Penny often played a variation of this game with her students in the library using multiple almanacs. The student who found the information in the shortest amount of time was the winner.

Skills Developed: In the upper grades of elementary school, the ability to use reference materials is very important, as is the ability to determine which type of materials to use for a specific task. Most schoolchildren are unfamiliar with almanacs and don't know how much information is available in them. This game gives your child practice in using an almanac, a book he will be able to use in projects and report writing in school. Any time you can widen the scope of his information about the resources available, take advantage of the opportunity.

Write Now

Helping Your Child Develop Writing Skills

n our society, a person is judged by his ability to use language effectively, organize thoughts, and express himself. As your child's spoken language improves, so will the way people regard him. Think of the child you see in the grocery store who points instead of asking for what he wants. We form an immediate impression—right or wrong—of his intelligence.

Once your child enters school, he will need to apply his language skills in a more advanced way. His teachers will expect him not only to speak clearly, but also to develop an ability to write. Writing requires a more advanced level of language and thought. However, many abilities have to come together before your child can actually begin to write as a means of expression.

Before he can even begin to write, he must be able to hold a pencil or a crayon. It takes a lot of practice with scribbling and making shapes before he can begin to make letters. He also has to understand oral language. A major breakthrough in the writing process comes when he learns that writing is spoken language in written form.

Sometimes children are reluctant to put words on paper because they are not sure of the exact spelling or because they might be given a poor grade as a result of faulty punctuation or a forgotten capital letter. But if we tell our children that we are interested in the content of the writing, not the mechanics, we allow them to shine in terms of creativity and imagination. Spelling, capitalization, and punctuation skills will be introduced and drilled in your child's classroom. When your child writes at home, however, let him be as creative with his spelling as he is with his content. This may be difficult for you at first, but you will find your child will be more expressive when allowed some freedom from traditional rules.

Although we all want our children to learn to spell correctly, invented spelling (spelling words the way they sound) improves and practices phonemic awareness. This reinforces concepts that help with both reading and writing.

That doesn't mean spelling is unimportant. In fact, we have included some games that will work on your child's spelling skills. And, of course, you will reinforce your child's spelling when you help him with his homework.

When children are allowed to express themselves freely, there are no right or wrong answers. Through the process of writing, your child not only learns how to write but also has the opportunity to explore ideas and feelings. He becomes more alert to his environment and is better able to remember what he has written. To be able to produce a piece of written work that is praised for its creativity and content is a tremendous esteem builder. And self-esteem, in turn, is very important to the writing process.

An unwise editor told Louisa May Alcott she would never be able to write anything that would appeal to the general public. It is lucky for us that she did not give up, but determination in the face of such negativity is rare. We do not want our children to experience this type of negativity. We want them to feel good about their written work and about their creativity. People enjoy doing what they do well. When we help our children succeed, they naturally want to continue the process.

Unfortunately, there is not enough encouragement for this type of activity in our elementary schools. Writing was once an integral part of the elementary school day. It was woven into all the content areas. Some enlightened school systems have made "writing through the curriculum" part of their strategy to improve writing skills, but many school systems now teach writing as a separate course with little relationship to the child's other school activities. These skills cannot be taught in isolation.

So how can we help our children? The Department of Education study *What Works* states, "Children who are encouraged to draw and scribble 'stories' at an early age will later learn to compose more easily, more effectively, and with greater confidence than children who do not have this encouragement." They found that children became more effective writers when they were encouraged to choose their own topics and to write about them.

One of the most important writing activities you can do with your child is simply to have him write. Young children love to show off what they have done when they feel their work is appreciated. How many of his talents are displayed on your refrigerator right now?

Children get to display their accomplishments with pride when they create their own books. They enjoy making books, and they love to read them to their parents, grandparents, neighbors, or anyone else who drops by. And the books can provide a memorable scrapbook for you.

Provide your child with blank pieces of paper, cardboard, file folders, or any materials you have around the house. Encourage him to draw a picture on each page and to write a sentence or two about each picture. Elementary school children love any excuse to draw. The pictures can be sequenced to create a story, or each page can shine independently. As your child's skills develop, encourage him to include more words than pictures. When complete, these books can be enjoyed over and over and will provide a variation for read-aloud time. One of Cheryl's prized possessions is a book created by her five-year-old about his sneakers. On the first page, he drew a picture of a brand-new pair of shoes. *New*, he wrote. The second page showed the same pair of shoes following an adventure in a mud puddle—*dirty*. He illustrated page 3 with the sneakers going into the washing machine—*help*, he wrote. On page 4, the sneakers were as new as on page 1—*new again*. It might have been an advertisement for a laundry detergent! When Cheryl read the book again recently, she was warmed to notice it had been dedicated to Mom and Dad.

The activities in this book recognize that children cannot be hurried through the stages of development, but they can be encouraged to experiment as much as possible within each stage to prepare for the next. The activities in this chapter do not focus on the mechanics of writing. There are no punctuation drills or capitalization quizzes. Instead, these games emphasize the creative aspects of writing and thinking skills. As your child writes, he will reach for the mechanical skills (capitalization, punctuation, complete sentence formation) he needs. You can help him then.

If your child is not developmentally ready to put letters on paper, he can still participate in activities that require writing by having an adult or older child record his thoughts. The thought organization process will be the same, but the mechanical act of putting the words on the paper will be left for later development. If he can form the letters, have him write the words so he can read them back later.

The skills emphasized in these games include explaining, generalizing, predicting, imagining, defending, inferring, and summarizing. These are the skills your child will need to become a creative thinker and a creative writer. So sharpen those pencils, and have a great time!

hat Is It?

Purpose: This game encourages your child to use language to meet her needs.

Materials Needed: No special materials are needed. This game can be played any time you are waiting with your child.

Number of Players: 2 or more

Time: Allow 5 minutes for each round.

How to Play: The object of the game is for the opponents to guess a secret object chosen by a given player. Present this game as an activity for spies. You have to be a good "looker" as well as a good listener, and you must be able to keep a secret. One player at a time chooses an object in the room but keeps her choice a secret. Opponents take turns asking yes/no questions to receive clues about the location or the identity of the object. The player who correctly guesses the mystery object wins.

Example: In a restaurant, the item might be the saltshaker. Questions might include "Is it on a person?" "Is it on the floor?" "Is it on the wall?" "Do we use it for eating?" and "Would I want to take it to school?"

Modifications for Older Children: If you are playing with older children, or if you are in a car where everything is going by quickly, you can use secret objects that can't be seen. This encourages players to rely more on their imagination and makes everyone more creative in choosing the secret objects.

Hints and Variations: Use discretion in limiting a round if it appears that no one is going to be able to guess the object. In that case, the person who chose the object becomes the winner, since she was able to stump the other players.

Skills Developed: Before your child can learn to write, she must be able to observe, think, and translate her thoughts into words. The skill of observing what is around her makes a child more aware of her environment and its effect on her. She must think about those observations before she can translate her thoughts into clear sentences.

This activity encourages the child to look critically at all items around her. If it is her turn to choose an object, she must try to determine which object might be the most difficult to guess. If she is the guesser, she must try to predict the other players' choices, keenly observe all items around her, and form critical questions that will help her discover the secret object. When she is able to formulate a question, she is using language to get the information she needs to win the game.

Add-Ons

Purpose: This game provides practice in creating descriptive and unusual sentences.

Materials Needed: To play, you will need paper and pencils.

Number of Players: Most fun with 3 or 4 players (also enjoyable for 2 people)

Time: Allow 15 to 30 minutes.

How to Play: In this game, the object is to add words to a given sentence to make a new sentence. The first player says a two-word sentence, which contains a noun and a verb—for example, *Girls eat.*

Each player, including the presenting player, writes a sentence using those two words and as many other words as possible to create a more elaborate sentence. Players could add words that tell how many, how large, what shape, what color, when, where, how, what, and so on. The sentence might become, *Two skinny girls eat round, yellow Popsicles at the county fair.* Each player receives 1 point for each word that is added appropriately to the sentence, and the player with the most points wins. Play continues as the next player says a two-word sentence.

Modifications for Older Children: Older children, with their expanded vocabularies, will write more-developed sentences. You may have them add only adjectives and adverbs, reinforcing that concept.

Hints and Variations: For younger players, and in situations where you are without pencil and paper, each player, in turn, adds a word or words to the sentence to create a new sentence without writing anything down. Play continues until no one is able to add new words. The winner is the player who adds the last word. The sentences given at each turn must be complete. For example, building on *Girls eat*, the first turn could be *Two girls eat*, then *Two girls eat Popsicles*, then *Two skinny girls eat Popsicles*, and so on.

Be careful not to overuse any particular type of word. If you allow too many color words, for example, the sentence could go on forever. We learned this the hard way. In one of Cheryl's classes, a student took the sentence *Many balloons flew* and created *Many yellow, blue, purple, black, red, brown, and pink balloons flew* before she invoked a two-color rule.

Skills Developed: The game encourages your child to extend a given sentence by using information he has learned from different sources. He will need to follow a logical sequence while experimenting with words and adding on to sentences. He will also need to visualize situations in his mind in order to describe these situations. This is a skill that is difficult for most children because television has begun to do the visualizing for them, leaving little to their imagination. This activity will encourage children to create their own pictures in their heads.

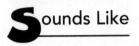ounds Like

Purpose: This game provides practice in categorizing words by beginning sounds.

Materials Needed: For this game, you need paper, pencils, and a timer.

Number of Players: Any number

Time: Allow 15 to 30 minutes for several rounds.

How to Play: The object of this game is to list as many words as possible that begin with a particular sound. One player takes a turn presenting a letter sound or a short blend (/sh/, /st/, /ch/) to the other players. All players, including the presenter, write as many words as they can think of in 3 minutes that begin with that sound. For example, if the letter sound chosen is /k/, players could list *cat*, *car*, and *kitten*. If the letter sound chosen is /s/, players could list *sea*, *soup*, and *celery*. At the end of the time, each player reads her list, and all words that appear on more than one list are eliminated. Points are given for any word that is not on any other list. Play continues with each player taking a turn as presenter. After the final round, the player with the most points wins.

Modifications for Older Children: Spelling should count when older children play this game. You might also want your older child to use longer words, maybe ruling that all words must be at least five letters long.

Hints and Variations: Unless you are playing with older children, spelling does not count as long as your child can read the word herself. Accept any approximation. Adjust the writing time to the ages of the players. Younger children might need longer than 3 minutes, and older children may need less time. You will be able to tell how much time is needed after you play once or twice.

For younger children, you can be the recorder, or younger and older children can play in teams. Here is another place you can use your child's vocabulary words as a starting point for the activity. You can also change the activity so that the words written have to have the same ending, rather than beginning, sound as the clue word. They would not have to rhyme, but merely end with the same final letter sound—*word, hard, forward, fried*.

Skills Developed: This game motivates your child to think of words she knows and to analyze them to determine whether they fit into a particular sound pattern. She will develop her attentiveness to words and will be able to break them into beginning and ending sounds.

Please Put Words in My Mouth

Purpose: In this game, your child practices creating sentences.

Materials Needed: You will need comic strips without words (or with words cut off or whited out), pencils, and paper.

Number of Players: 3 or more

Time: Allow 10 to 20 minutes.

How to Play: The object of the game is to create complete sentences to describe or accompany a picture. Begin with comic strips from the newspaper or from a comic book. Use one frame of the strip for each round of the game. All players are shown the same frame, and they must write a complete sentence of dialogue appropriate to the picture. When all the sentences are written, the players read them aloud and vote on which sentence best describes the situation creatively.

Modifications for Older Children: Children of all ages enjoy this game. Sometimes our older child will come up with the funniest, most clever sentences, but younger children also can come up with some hilarious descriptions.

Hints and Variations: With younger children, you can play in teams, or you and an older child could help a younger one create sentences. This is a good game for children who have difficulty with reading and writing skills because creativity is the most important component of the game.

Your child's dialogue might describe the situation, or it may offer a funny explanation for what is happening in the strip. The more creative the dialogue, the more fun this game becomes. For example, when Cheryl played with her son, they used a frame showing a snowball chasing Garfield down the hill. Her sentence (*Garfield is running down the hill, being chased by a giant snowball*) was accurate, but her son's sentence (*A snowball from space raced Garfield to the house for dinner*) was much funnier.

Save comic strips for several days so that you will have many choices to use for the game. If you are playing with 2 players, each player can choose his own comic strip and write as many sentences as possible to create a short paragraph suggesting what the character is saying. This becomes more of a shared experience than a competitive game and is a fun way for you to help your child develop his writing skills. You might even enjoy creating dialogue together for the same comic strip.

Skills Developed: Your child's attention span and interpretation skills will become more developed with this game. It provides practice in creating complete sentences as part of a story. Please Put Words in My Mouth will help your child analyze situations and become more aware of cause and effect. The skills developed with this game will help your child better understand the charts, graphs, and pictures often featured in textbooks.

This game reinforces the values of sportsmanship and fair play, since the winner is determined by a vote of the other players. It also requires a sense of humor.

Frances's License to Play

Purpose: This game encourages your child to use complete sentences and provides practice in sentence building.

Materials Needed: You need no special materials, but players must be in view of car license plates.

Number of Players: 2 or a carful

Time: Allow 5 minutes or less for each round.

How to Play: The object of the game is to be the first player to create a complete sentence using the letters on a car license plate as the first letter of each of the words in the sentence. One player notices a license plate that contains two or more letters and announces the letters to the other players. All players, as soon as possible, call out complete sentences made up of words that begin with the letters as they appear on the license plate. For example, BPA could stand for *Boys pick apples.* The first player to arrive at a complete sentence can choose the next plate.

Modifications for Older Children: Older children with more language experience will probably be able to come up with sentences more quickly than your younger child. Older children could be required to use a particular part of speech. For example, each sentence must have an adverb.

Hints and Variations: Give yourself a handicap by trying to make your sentence more complex than those your child might create. This will allow your child a chance to win and will provide an example of the type of sentence you hope she will eventually begin to create. By using descriptive words in your sentences, you show how to use words to make sentences more colorful—for example, *Boys play appropriately*. You might want to exempt the driver from choosing the license plate, since she should be spending her time looking at the road!

Skills Developed: The ability to respond in complete sentences is the way we inform others of what we know and understand. In school, a child must write spelling words and answer test and discussion questions in complete sentences. In most cases, she will have some information (the spelling word or the clues of the question), but she will have to generate the rest of the sentence herself.

This activity encourages your child to complete sentences relying mainly on her inner resources with very few guidelines. She will have to use nouns and verbs even if she doesn't yet know what they are. The ability to generate sentences in order to express ourselves enables us to make ourselves understood. When your child sees that she can have her needs met through language, it gives her the confidence she'll need to venture out into the world.

Sentence Fun

Purpose: This game provides practice in creating sentences using specific, often unrelated words.

Materials Needed: To play, you will need pencils and paper.

Number of Players: 3 or more (or 2 players using the Hints and Variations)

Time: Allow 15 to 30 minutes.

How to Play: The object of the game is to create a complete sentence using predetermined words. One player takes a turn naming three words that everyone must use in creating a sentence. These words do not have to relate to one another. In fact, the game is most challenging and fun when they do not relate. Everyone, including the presenting player, creates a sentence using those three words and as many other words as he wants in order to make a creative sentence. For example, the three words might be *rain, leaf, bottle.* A sentence using these words could be as simple as *I watched the rain fall on a leaf and a bottle* or as complex as *While I was walking in the rain, I slipped on a leaf and fell on a bottle.* Each player reads his sentence aloud, and everyone votes on the most creative sentence that makes sense. The player whose sentence is chosen is the winner of the round. Continue with a new set of words, giving each player a chance to be presenter.

Modifications for Older Children: Older children can take their words from their school spelling lists or vocabulary from their science or social studies lessons. This helps them reinforce their spelling and vocabulary skills and gives them an opportunity to use the new words in sentences.

Hints and Variations: When playing with younger children, have them say the sentence aloud without having to write it down. This will also increase the competition because the other players hear what the previous player has said and are challenged to come up with a better sentence. You could also play in teams, and you could do the writing for the younger child. The words can be chosen from school words, kitchen words, restaurant words, or words appropriate to any setting where the game is played. This game worked well for Penny while she was making dinner and all her children wanted her attention.

Without paper and pencil, this game becomes a great game to play while waiting at a restaurant or in a car. If you are playing with only 2 players, each player can present three words for the other player to use in making a sentence. Since there are only two of you, you can eliminate the vote. Everyone wins this way.

If you want to add the element of chance, play with a game board. Each player, in turn, presents three words to the next player, who must make a sentence using those words. The player who makes the sentence then rolls the dice and moves around the game board. If your child cannot come up with a sentence, gently suggest one to him, and see if he can come up with a variation of yours.

Skills Developed: Your child will explore the possible ways of combining words, resulting in the imaginative use of language. He will develop a better understanding of how words go together to create a complete sentence. This game provides an opportunity for you to teach your child to respect the rights and feelings of others. Sentence Fun encourages sportsmanship and fair play. The winner is determined by vote, and it is important for all players to realize that everyone is a winner if he is having a good time.

Blankety Blanks

Purpose: This game provides practice in developing sentences with creativity and imagination.

Materials Needed: You will need paper and pencils.

Number of Players: At least 2 (best with more than 2 players)

Time: Allow 10 to 20 minutes.

How to Play: The objective is to identify what word the presenting player left out of a sentence. The presenter writes a sentence she has created, leaving out one word that is important to the sentence. For example, the sentence might be *Joe was so tired he put his* _____ *on the table*. On separate pieces of paper, each player then writes one word that could go in the blank space. On her piece of paper, the presenting player writes the word she removed. The players read their chosen words aloud, and each player who matches the word of the presenting player receives 1 point. If no one matches the presenter, he or she gets 1 point. The game continues with a new presenter and a new sentence. The player with the most points wins.

Modifications for Older Players: This game provides older children with the opportunity to be especially creative. They can come up with some very funny sentences when playing this game and selecting which word to omit.

Hints and Variations: This game can be played without writing the sentence. The creation of the sentence with the missing element is more important than the actual writing. You don't want to make your child uncomfortable if she is unable to write or spell correctly, and it is often easier for a young child to create a sentence orally than to write it down. She should write the one word to fill in the blank, however.

A variation of this game for only 2 players would be for each player to write as many words as possible to fill in the blank. Identical responses are eliminated, and players get 1 point for each unique and logical response. Another variation for 2 or more players is for each player, in turn, to say a word that could fill in the blank. The last player to be able to suggest an appropriate word is the winner. This will allow your child to use her powers of persuasion to convince you that her word makes sense.

Skills Developed: This game provides opportunities for sentence development and allows your child to explore and play with words and word combinations with a strategy in mind. She will write a sentence and then eliminate one of the words. She will need to think of possible words that can be used in her created sentence, and she must anticipate which words other players might use.

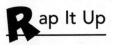 ap It Up

Purpose: Here's another game that encourages practice in making sentences while allowing your child to be creative and imaginative.

Materials Needed: You will need paper and pencils.

Number of Players: Any number

Time: Allow 15 to 30 minutes.

How to Play: The object of the game is to create sentences that rhyme. Players take turns starting the rhyme. The first player writes a sentence, which becomes the first line of a poem. Each player, in turn, adds a line that follows the idea of the first sentence. The final word must rhyme with the end of the previous sentence. For example, if the first line is *I see a bear*, the next line might be *He had no hair.* The players continue adding additional lines until a player is unable to add any more. The last player to add a line gets 1 point. The player with the most points is the winner. If no one can add a second line to the poem, the player who started the poem receives 1 point.

The rhyming style is one young people are very familiar with, since they hear rap singers rhyme each day on the radio.

Modifications for Older Children: This game can make homework fun when your child uses spelling words in each line of the poem.

Hints and Variations: With younger children, you can play this game without actually writing anything down. Each player would say his line instead of writing it. The goal is to create a sentence with a final word that rhymes. Remember, writing is simply talk written down. This is a good way to come up with a personalized message to send as a birthday or get-well card, and your child could add a picture to go along with the poem. Cheryl's boys hated to write thank-you notes, and this was one way they could do it together and have fun.

To get the creative juices flowing, you could even start with the picture drawing and have the poem relate to the picture. It might also be fun to read some rhymes during your read-aloud time as an introduction to this game. Many children's picture books are created in rhyme. It is also an opportunity to introduce your child to your favorite poets.

Skills Developed: This game helps reinforce the rhyming skills that are so important in reading readiness in kindergarten and first grade. Rhyming, writing, and reading in this way will help develop and reinforce phonemic awareness. Rap It Up also helps develop sentence-building skills. Your child can be creative and imaginative in building sentences while he searches for rhyming patterns.

Comp and Con

Purpose: This game encourages vocabulary development and fosters an understanding of how things are alike and different.

Materials Needed: You will need paper and pencils.

Number of Players: 2 to 6

Time: Allow 15 to 30 minutes.

How to Play: In this game, players will list words or complete sentences that describe two objects. To begin with, one player names two objects. Each player then makes a list on a piece of paper of the ways in which the two objects are alike and how they are different. For example, the objects tree and ship are alike in that both float, are wooden, and can be tall. They are different in that trees do not carry people, trees are alive, and ships don't grow.

When all lists are finished, the players read their answers. Answers that are the same on more than one list are eliminated, and players receive 1 point for each idea that does not appear on another list. If there is a dispute about any of the similarities or differences, the player must defend her choice to the satisfaction of the other players. If your child can argue that a ship and a tree are alike because they both make people happy, let her use her persuasive language skills to justify the comparison. Play continues with the players taking turns naming the pairs of objects.

Modifications for Older Children: This skill is more highly developed in older children. It is probably best that this game not be played in multiage groups and that you play this game exclusively with your older child.

Hints and Variations: To play with younger children or while you are waiting for a meal or an appointment, you can also play this game without pencil and paper. In this variation, each player, in turn, names one way in which the objects are alike and one way in which they are different. The last player to be able to compare and contrast the objects is the winner. The power of persuasion is also very useful when you play this way.

Skills Developed: Comp and Con encourages your child to come up with descriptive words that fit a pair of objects such as tree/ship, television/VCR. This will help develop a better understanding of the meanings of words and how they relate to other words. Your child will see that the things around us have many different features.

Where Does It Belong?

Purpose: This is another game that provides practice in categorization skills.

Materials Needed: You will need pencils and paper.

Number of Players: 2 to 4

Time: Allow 15 to 20 minutes.

How to Play: The object of this game is to create a list of words that belong in a particular category and do not appear on the other players' lists. One player takes a turn naming a category—dogs, large things, weather. All players, including the presenting player, write as many items as they can that belong to that category. For example, using the category of dogs, a list might include huskies, terriers, mutts, goldens.

When the lists are complete, each player reads his list. Items that appear on more than one list are eliminated. Players receive 1 point for each word that is not on any other list. If a player includes an item in a category that the other players feel does not belong, the player must defend his choice to the satisfaction of the other players. Play continues as the players take turns selecting categories. Whoever has the highest point total wins.

Modifications for Older Children: With older children, use items from the news as the categories. This will keep them up-to-date on current events and make them more aware of the world around them.

Hints and Variations: Do not make correct spelling a part of this game. Allow your child to be just as creative in his spelling as in his choice of words. Cheryl's sons could come up with many examples they couldn't spell. If they had worried about spelling, she would have missed out on *wrecked car* in the flat category or *gorilla* in the strong category. Be open to unusual responses. If your child can defend George Bush as an example of a plant, give credit for it. You want to encourage imagination.

If you are playing with younger children, play in teams, so they will not be excluded by the inability to write. Feel free to offer suggestions of possible categories, but be sure to offer more than one idea so the presenting player can choose the one he wants to use. Your child must feel that he has some control over the direction of the game in order to feel a part of it.

Skills Developed: Where Does It Belong? is similar to Picka in Chapter 2 and provides another example that writing is simply talk written down. This game helps your child expand his vocabulary and make generalizations about words and ideas. It encourages him to be more alert to his environment in order to build up ideas for future sessions of the game. While playing, he will be developing a new way of noticing things in his world, because he will begin to relate each thing he sees to a category—for instance, people, blue things, things made of glass. He may have to defend his choice of a particular item as part of a category, and this will improve his thinking skills.

Descriptions

Purpose: This game motivates your child to use language creatively.

Materials Needed: To play, you will need pictures, pencils, paper, and a timer. Also, you need to gather magazine or newspaper pictures or family photos.

Number of Players: 2 or more

Time: Allow 15 to 20 minutes.

How to Play: The object of the game is to describe a picture by using words that are not used by any other players. Choose a picture from a magazine or family album. Each player may look at it for 1 minute. Each player then makes a list of words that describe the picture. When all lists are complete, the words on the lists are read off, and all the words that appear on more than one list are eliminated. If words on a list do not seem to apply to the picture, give the player an opportunity to explain why she chose each word. For example, in a picture of children jumping rope, describing words might be *happy, playful, joyful, smiling*. A child using the word *hot* could argue that the children would not be wearing shorts if it were not hot outside. Limit responses to individual descriptive words, since it is very difficult to compare phrases objectively. Each player receives 1 point for each word on her list that was not on any other list. The player with the most points wins.

Modifications for Older Children: When you play with older children, use pictures from the newspaper. Coming up with descriptive words for current events will strengthen their awareness of the world around them.

Hints and Variations: If you are playing with younger children, each player could say aloud a word that describes the picture. The last to name a describing word is the winner. You or an older child might want to write down all players' words to guard against duplication. This game is a good opportunity to use pictures in schoolbooks to help your child review her homework.

Be careful if choosing a picture of yourself. We were surprised by some of the describing words our children used!

Skills Developed: This game encourages your child to be more attentive to her environment and to develop a facility with words that describe what she sees. She must grasp the meaning of pictures that have no words and translate that understanding to language. She will also be listening to words you use and will thus develop her vocabulary. When lists of words are compared, players might have to defend their choices, and they will need to use language effectively to prove their point.

atterns

Purpose: This game provides practice in creating sentences that follow a prescribed pattern.

Materials Needed: This game requires a game board, die, paper, and pencils.

Number of Players: 2 to 4

Time: Allow 30 minutes.

How to Play: The object of the game is to create sentences using a specific series of letters for the beginning letter of each word in the sentence. The first player writes a series of letters and shows it to the player to his left. The series can be in alphabetical order (A, B, C, D), the letters of his name (E, R, I, C), or any letters the player wants to use. The number of letters is determined by the players at the beginning of the game.

The next player must create a sentence using the letters provided—for example, *A boy can drive* (A, B, C, D) or *Eagles ride in clouds* (E, R, I, C). If he forms a sentence correctly, he rolls the die and moves around the game board. The player who rolls the die then presents a series of letters to the player to his left, who uses the series to create a sentence. Play continues until someone completes his way around the board.

Using the game board adds an element of chance to the game and provides the younger player with an equal opportunity to win.

This game is similar to Frances's License to Play, described earlier in this chapter, except that here your child creates the letter pattern and writes down the sentences. Also, sentences will probably be much longer in Patterns, as most license plates have only a few letters.

Modifications for Older Children: When playing with older children, have them use more letters to create their sentences.

Hints and Variations: Tailor the length of the sentences to the age of your child. For younger children, use a three-letter series. If children cannot yet write, allow them to create their sentences orally, or you can play in teams with you writing the sentence your child creates.

Skills Developed: Patterns encourages your child to follow a logical, sequential order while experimenting with word combinations. He will develop his originality and creativity and find ways to express his ideas. Because he will be creating sentences based on a specific sequence, which is presented by another player, the order imposed by this game will increase his attention to detail.

Creative Critiquers

Purpose: This game will motivate your child to use her sentence-making skills as she watches television in a more creative way.

Materials Needed: Surprise, this game is played in front of the television! You will also need paper and pencils.

Number of Players: Minimum of 2 (the more, the merrier—an excellent game for the entire family)

Time: Allow 15 to 20 minutes in addition to the time spent watching the television program.

How to Play: The object of the game is to create a review of a television program, including as many details and as much analysis as possible. Players must agree to watch the same program. Each player can decide for herself whether she will keep the pencil and paper out during the show and take notes, or whether she will rely on her memory of the total program. (If you are playing with your child, encourage her to keep notes while you rely on memory.) At the end of the program, each player writes a summary of the program, using as many details as possible. She makes judgments, both positive and negative, about the parts of the show that were meaningful to her. For example, after watching any family show, the summary may include a description of the people and their home, as well as whether the situation was one that might happen in your home. Your child might compare how a situation was handled on the television program with how it might have been handled in your home.

Critiques are compared. Scoring here is subjective. If you feel it is necessary to declare a winner, base your decision on the total number of details.

Modifications for Older Children: Determine beforehand what qualities you will be looking for—instances of humor or conflict, for example. This will give you an opportunity to discuss family issues.

Hints and Variations: Younger children can be allowed to give their summaries orally after you have written yours. Another variation would allow each player to earn points for each object she noticed that no one else saw. This variation is easier for younger children because they can list objects they noticed, rather than events. Each player reads her list, and duplicate items are eliminated. To play without any writing at all, each player states an object or event, in turn, and the last player to remember a detail is declared the winner.

Children often enjoy analyzing commercials. Since commercials are shorter than an entire program, the activity can be done quickly if time is an issue.

Skills Developed: This game provides practice with critical thinking, analyzing, and summarizing. It develops the ability to look at a whole situation and break it down into its parts. Your child will have to be attentive to details and alert to how those details relate to each other and to the entire program. It should produce a more critical television viewer and make your child more selective. This game could inspire your child to one day become a screenwriter or film critic.

 **N**ame It

Purpose: This game helps your child develop vocabulary and the powers of observation.

Materials Needed: This game requires paper and pencils.

Number of Players: 2 to 4

Time: Allow 15 to 30 minutes.

How to Play: The object of the game is to use unique words to describe another player. Each player's name, in turn, is used for the activity. Each player writes the first and last names down the left side of a piece of paper:

M	Music lover
I	Ice cream eater
C	Chummy
H	Hairy
A	Amiable
E	Exciting
L	Lively
R	Rowdy
O	Ornery
S	Sincere
S	Smiling

Next to each letter, each player writes a word or phrase that begins with the letter and that describes the person whose name is being used. No insulting terms are allowed. At the end of the allotted time, each player reads the words or phrases he has written. All entries that are on more than one list are eliminated. Players receive 1 point for each word or phrase that was not used by any of the other players. The player with the most points wins.

Modifications for Older Players: With older children, you might also describe objects. This is much more abstract and difficult. For example, in describing a chair, you might write, "**C**lose to the floor, **h**ard, **a**t the table, **i**n the living room, **r**estful."

Hints and Variations: If, after playing this game often, you have used the names of the entire family and circle of friends, use the name of a person in the neighborhood, in the news, or on television. Since you do not count spelling, each child should read his own list.

Skills Developed: This game encourages your child to recognize how words can express character traits and how those traits can apply to a particular individual. For example, the word *moody* might make us think of someone we know who is happy one minute and grumpy the next. The ability to find the perfect words to describe a person or situation is a skill he will use throughout school while searching for the best word to use in a report or a project. Your child will develop his visual attention skills as he concentrates on an individual's particular characteristics and then labels the characteristics on his list. He might one day use this talent if he becomes a psychologist, a portrait painter, a poet, or a private detective.

Heads Up

Purpose: Heads Up provides practice with spelling and with vocabulary development.

Materials Needed: To play, you will need paper, pencils, and a dictionary.

Number of Players: 2 to 4

Time: Allow 15 to 30 minutes.

How to Play: The object of the game is to fill in a chart with words that are different from the words used by other players. One player chooses a four-, five-, or six-letter guide word. All players write the guide word vertically in both the left and the right margins of their sheet of paper. In the left margin, they spell the word from top to bottom, and in the right margin, they write it from bottom to top.

Each player then writes words that fit horizontally into the chart created by the letters. For example, if the word *stop* is written up and down the margins, the first word filled in must begin with *S* and end with *P*. The second word must begin with *T* and end with *O*, and so on:

S	tam	P
T	emp	O
O	bjec	T
P	as	S

Scattergories everbury

Players may use words they know, or they may use a dictionary to find words to fit the pattern. When they use a dictionary, they must be able to pronounce the words they choose.

When all lists are complete, the players compare lists. Words that are on more than one list are eliminated. Players receive 1 point for any word remaining on their list. The player with the most points wins.

Modifications for Older Children: Older children can work with longer words for the target word. They can also create more than one word for each pair.

Hints and Variations: Use this game to help your child study for spelling by using spelling words as the guide words. Try to keep your words at a level close to your child's, so she will have an opportunity to win. You can do this by limiting your words to those found in a children's dictionary or by using ones that are the length she might use.

Skills Developed: Most children can use practice in reinforcing spelling and vocabulary. With this game, your child will have to call to mind or look up words that fit a particular spelling pattern. Looking up words exposes her to new vocabulary, and placing words on the chart makes her more aware of spelling patterns. This game also helps with one of the most difficult phonemic awareness skills: helping children focus on the sounds in the middle of words.

ebus

Purpose: This game gives your child practice in creating complete sentences while translating the spoken word into pictures.

Materials Needed: You will need pencils or crayons and paper.

Number of Players: 3 to 6

Time: Allow 15 to 30 minutes.

How to Play: The object of the game is to create a sentence with drawings or individual numbers or letters replacing each of the words. One player creates a sentence and writes the sentence by using pictures, numbers, or letters instead of using the words themselves. For example, *I can see you* would look like this: 👁 🛢 C U . The other players try to read the sentence correctly by shouting out what they think the sentence says. The first player to guess the actual sentence is the winner and has the opportunity to create the next clue sentence. If no one is able to read the sentence, the person who presented it is the winner and gets another chance to present.

Modifications for Older Children: Many older children have seen examples of rebus books, so they may already have a basic understanding of how this game works. They will be able to come up with many more representative pictures than younger children, so their sentences can be longer and more complex.

Hints and Variations: For younger players, make a chart of the possible rebus (picture) clues, and keep it within everyone's sight. Use any combination of picture clues that the players can agree upon. Make sure you allow many action words (verbs), so you will have enough to choose from. For example, *run* could be 🏃. Be sure the drawings are as simple as possible, so the less artistic child won't be intimidated.

Since Cheryl's artistic skills are not her strong point, she and her boys could often laugh at her picture clues. It was a good way for the boys to see that, in some areas at least, children have stronger skills than their parents.

Skills Developed: This game motivates your child to create a complete sentence in his head and to imagine what it would look like represented by drawings. When your child conveys an idea using drawings rather than words, he gains some insight into ways to present material in nonverbal forms, such as charts or illustrations. This activity helps develop the ability to break down information into its parts and then successfully put the pieces together in an innovative way. For example, the word *canteen* might be represented by a drawing of a can and a teenager together.

This is also a great way to improve visual memory, because the player who remembers the fastest what the picture clues represent will usually be the one to solve the sentence first.

Ask Me a Question

Purpose: This game helps your child develop the skill of question formation.

Materials Needed: To play, you will need paper and pencils.

Number of Players: 2 to 6

Time: Allow 15 to 30 minutes.

How to Play: The object of the game is to create word problems. One child creates, writes, and then presents a math problem. The problem presented could be 2 + 2 = 4. The player to her left makes up a story that uses that problem and asks a question about the story. For example, the story and question could be, "There are two children playing this game. Two more children come over to play. How many children would be playing?" For each successful story, give 1 point. If the story is incorrect or the player could not create a story, the player who presented the problem receives 1 point. Play continues with everyone taking turns presenting a problem. The player with the most points at the end of the allotted time wins.

Modifications for Older Children: Older children should be required to use more than one math process in each of their sentences. For example, the problem could be $2 \times 2 - 3 = 1$. The story problem could be "Two cats each had two kittens. Three of the kittens were adopted. How many kittens were left?"

Hints and Variations: For play with younger children or at a time when pencil and paper are unavailable, allow the players to present the problem orally. This is a good game to play while waiting at a restaurant or for a doctor's appointment. You can even use it to an advantage when tempers are short and everyone is impatient.

Use your child's math homework to find problems on which to base your stories. This is a good way to help her remember her math facts. Don't use problems that are too hard for your child. You are not trying to teach her to multiply. You are trying to help her learn to form questions while reinforcing the skills she is learning at school.

When encouraged to use their hobbies and interests as material for their stories, Cheryl's boys often came up with more complicated stories than she would have imagined possible. Even simple math facts were interpreted creatively. Here is what her young son's response was when given the problem $1 + 1 + 2 = 4$: "During last week's baseball game, Andy ended his batting slump. At first it seemed Andy would be sitting on the bench for the next game. His first time at bat, he struck out—again! He was really down but tried to remind himself that he was up against Chris, one of the Yachtsmen's best pitchers. As lead-off batter in the third inning, he got a single. That was a relief! The next player walked. 'Good eye!' his teammates yelled. That brought Travis to bat. He was the team's strongest hitter. He smacked the ball—a strong line drive to the outfield, and Andy slid into home plate. How many bases did Andy touch during the third inning?"

Skills Developed: Your child uses the skills of visualization and imagination to create a story based on a given math problem. As this game is the reverse of a mathematical word problem, it will help with writing as well as math skills. In a math word problem, your child reads a question about a situation and adds, subtracts, multiplies, or divides the numbers in it to arrive at an answer. In Ask Me a Question, she begins with the math problem and its answer and creates a question that represents those math facts. She must use words to express math concepts. She will begin to see more clearly how math and language are related and how understanding the language of math can help take some of the mystery out of the subject. This game is difficult to lose, fun to play, and encourages humorous responses.

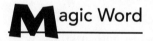agic Word

Purpose: Magic Word provides practice in spelling and vocabulary development.

Materials Needed: To play, you will need paper, pencils, and a dictionary (optional).

Number of Players: 2 to 4

Time: Allow at least 15 minutes.

How to Play: The object of the game is for each player to create a new word by changing a letter in a given word. One player chooses the original guide word to be used. This word is written on a piece of paper and shown to the other player. Each player, in turn, may change one letter in the word in order to create a new word. For example, if the guide word is *line*, the second player can change it to *mine*, the third can change it to *mile*, the fourth to *tile*, and so on. Each time the word is changed, the new one must be a real word and must be spelled correctly. The winner is the last player able to create a new word.

Modifications for Older Children: Older children can work with four- or five-letter words. At all ages, this kind of play can improve spelling and phonemic awareness.

Hints and Variations: This is a good way to work with spelling assignments and specific vocabulary from schoolbooks. Use the words from school as the given words to allow your child to play with his spelling or vocabulary homework.

Tailor the length of the word to the age of the child. Beginning readers could handle a three-letter word, such as changing *big* to *pig*, *pit*, *pot*. Include the nonreading child on a team with you to make him feel part of the game. This is also a way that you can justify instructing as you go.

It is possible to play without paper and pencils if you limit your words to three letters. It might also be a good idea for you to pick the guide word, because you want to be sure that it is a word with many options. Good four-letter words to begin with are those with a silent *e* at the end, those with *ai* in the middle, and those ending with *ig*, *an*, or *ar*. Let your child use a children's dictionary to help him come up with new words, and he will develop research skills at the same time.

Skills Developed: This game will help your child develop a better understanding of spelling rules and phonemic awareness. He will see similarities in spelling patterns as he creates new words from old ones—for example: *fat*, *hat*, or *sat* from *cat*. He will develop his ability to break down words into their letters and letter combinations.

He will also begin to visualize possible changes by manipulating the letter combinations in his mind.

ordy

Purpose: This game gives your child practice in comparing words based on similarities in spelling.

Materials Needed: This game requires paper and pencils.

Number of Players: 2 to 4

Time: Allow 20 to 30 minutes.

How to Play: The object of the game is to discover your opponent's secret word. One player, the presenter, writes a word on a piece of paper and conceals it from the other players. The presenter gives only one clue about the secret word: the number of letters it contains. The other players, in turn, guess words that have the same number of letters. The presenter lets them know if any of the letters in the guessed word are the same as those in the secret word, but tells only how many.

The process sounds complicated, but it's very simple. It goes like this: The presenting player chooses the secret word *time*. She tells the other players that her secret word has four letters. Each player draws four blanks at the top of her paper. The first player might guess *milk*. All players list the letters *M, I, L, K* under their blanks:

———   ———   ———   ———

M   I   L   K

The presenter tells the first player that the secret word and *milk* have two letters in common. She does not tell her which letters. The next player tries to think of a word that has at least two of the letters found in milk. She might guess *lock*, and the players would write that word beneath *milk*:

				Number of correct letters
__	__	__	__	
M	I	L	K	2
L	O	C	K	0

When the presenting player says none of the letters in *lock* are contained in the secret word, the players know that the *L* and *K* in *milk* are not in the secret word either, so *M* and *I* must be two of the letters found in the secret word. They work this out on their papers by crossing out the letters definitely not in the secret word and by placing the letters definitely in the secret word above the blanks at the top, one letter per blank.

M	*I*			Number of correct letters
__	__	__	__	
M	I	L	K	2
L	O	C	K	0

Now the players know two of the letters, but they still don't know where the letters fall in the secret word. The next player chooses a word that contains both *M* and *I*—for example, *dime*. The presenting player announces that *dime* contains three of the letters in the secret word. Again, players do not know if the secret word contains the *E* or the *D*. So the next player guesses a word containing either an *E* or a *D*, plus the *I*, the *M*, and one of the letters definitely out—*lime*. The players know the *E* is contained in the secret word, because *I* has already been eliminated. The worksheet is then updated:

M	I	E		Number of correct letters
—	—	—	—	
M	I	L	K	2
L	O	C	K	0
D	I	M	E	3
L	I	M	E	3

Now the players know three of the four letters, but they still do not know the order of the letters. The next player guesses a word containing the three known letters and one additional new letter. She might guess *mine* or *mike* or the correct word, *time*. If she does not guess the correct word, the next player gets a chance. If the player guesses a word with four correct letters—*mite*—the presenting player tells her the letters are correct but in the wrong order. The guesser gets one more chance to guess. The player to guess the secret word is the winner.

Whew! It usually takes one round of this game to become comfortable with the format, but it is well worth the effort.

Modifications for Older Children: Obviously, this game is designed for older children and needs no modification.

Hints and Variations: With only 2 players, each player chooses a word for the other player to discover. Keep track of how many guesses it takes each player to figure out the secret word. The player who guesses in the fewest number of turns wins. Be sure to keep the length and difficulty of the words appropriate to the age of the child. You can get a good idea of words to use from their schoolbooks. You could also make this game a creative way to get them to do their spelling homework. Use their spelling words, or words with the same spelling pattern, as your secret word. For example, if the spelling list contains words with *or* in them such as *corn*, also use other words with *or*—*torn* or *fork*.

To make this game easier for younger children, allow the presenting player to tell which letters of the guessed word are in the secret word. For example, if the secret word is *time* and the guess is *milk*, the presenter would disclose that *m* and *i* are in the secret word.

Skills Developed: In this game, your child is encouraged to think of words based on the letters they contain and the way the letters are combined. She will develop skills in categorizing words based on length and spelling rules. She will be improving her ability to spell without the drill of studying spelling words, as she sees how words often follow common patterns. The game also develops strong concentration skills.

Politics

Purpose: This game encourages your older child to analyze a picture and choose appropriate words to describe what she sees. The concepts involved would be too difficult for a younger child.

Materials Needed: This game requires political cartoons, paper, and pencils.

Number of Players: 2 to 6

Time: Allow 15 to 30 minutes.

How to Play: The object of the game is to list words describing a political cartoon. All players look at the same cartoon, and then each player lists words that suggest the emotions or ideas she felt were expressed in the cartoon. For example, a cartoon about a political election might make you think of words such as *decisions, confusion, political, democratic,* and the like. When all lists are complete, players read the words they have written, and all words that are on more than one list are eliminated. Players receive 1 point for each word that is not on any other list. If a word is challenged by the other players as being inappropriate to the cartoon, the player who used it must defend her choice to the satisfaction of the other players. The player with the most points wins.

Hints and Variations: Save political cartoons from newspapers for several days in order to play for more than one round. It is a good idea to have enough cartoons that all the players have some choice about the ones to use. Any time you give your child some responsibility in the decision-making process, the exercise will be more personal and will have a greater meaning for her.

Skills Developed: Report writing in the upper grades requires your child to understand a subject, develop opinions about it, analyze those opinions, and come to some conclusions. This game, on a much smaller scale, calls on those same skills. Your child will have to look at a picture, get meaning from what she sees, analyze the situation presented, and make some judgments. She then will have to write words to support her opinions and may also have to convince the other players that her judgment is correct.

Telegram

Purpose: This game provides practice in summarizing and in note taking and is designed for older children.

Materials Needed: To play, you will need a schoolbook, magazine, or newspaper, as well as paper and pencils.

Number of Players: 3 or more

Time: Allow 15 to 30 minutes.

How to Play: The object of the game is to rewrite a sentence in as few words as possible, keeping the meaning of the sentence clear. One player locates a sentence in a newspaper, book, or magazine and reads the sentence aloud to the other players. All players then rewrite the same sentence in as few words as possible. For example, *The Japanese government plans to export more cars to the United States* becomes

More Japanese cars coming to U.S. All players read their rewrites aloud and vote on which is the clearest using the fewest words. This game encourages good sportsmanship and fair play.

Hints and Variations: This could be a good way to help your child take homework notes. Use his schoolbook for the game, and have some fun while getting the homework done. He might think you are doing some of the work for him, but you are actually showing him, by example, an important study skill.

You could also make the game more like a telegram. Each player would start out with an imaginary amount of money, say, $2. Subtract 5 cents for each word used in the rewritten sentence. The person with the most money left at the end of the each round is the winner.

Skills Developed: This game will give your child a head start on the skills he will need in middle school and high school. He will need to be able to take notes on information he hears in class and reads at home. As parents, we usually don't give too much attention to note taking as a skill; we just expect our children to know how to do it. This game provides guidelines and encourages him to rewrite written information in a type of shorthand that will have meaning for him.

4

Count Me In

Helping Your Child Develop Math Skills

f Matthew took the train from Boston to Baltimore at 7:30 A.M. and the train traveled at 50 miles per hour but stopped in New York for a 30-minute layover, and if Danielle's train traveled from Columbus, Georgia, to Baltimore, leaving at 9:00 A.M., traveling directly at 75 miles per hour, and if the distance from Boston to Baltimore is one-third more than the distance from Columbus to New York, how old is Matthew's cat?

For many adults, word problems make no more sense than that. These adults have struggled with numbers since they were children. Frightened they will pass along their fears, they are uncomfortable trying to help their own children with math skills. Perhaps you are one of those adults. If so, fear not. Even if you are math phobic, you can help your child develop the thinking skills that are fundamental to success in mathematics, and you may even learn to enjoy math in the process.

For some, math comes easily. If you are comfortable with math and want to share your love of numbers and logical thought with your children, dive right in. This chapter is for you, too.

Children are not born with a fear of math. They love to investigate and to discover, and the process of discovery is uniquely satisfying. It is a real esteem booster for young children to tackle a challenge and solve it creatively.

A young child responds to math experiences based on what she sees around her. A child in the elementary grades can usually interpret information she sees and can arrive at a simple, logical conclusion. For example, if a kindergarten child knows that there are three snacks and four children in her group, she understands someone is going to have to share.

In the early elementary years, your child will learn the rote math skills of addition, subtraction, multiplication, and division. Often, however, a child can do a full page of problems that require one of these four processes, but when expected to determine which process to use in a word problem, she doesn't know where to begin. Math has a special language that tells us what to do with numbers. To decide which process to use and how to apply it, your child must understand that language. She needs to know that when a problem asks how many are left, she should subtract. When a problem asks how many there are altogether, she should add.

Math provides children with a method and a language for organizing information. We use math for comparing, ordering, predicting, and graphing. The goal of mathematical learning is to develop problem-solving abilities.

Issues surrounding a child's weekly allowance often present problem-solving opportunities. When Penny's older son's favorite ball was thrown into the ocean during a game with his friends, he needed to know how many weeks he would need to save his allowance before he could buy a new one.

Children acquire problem-solving skills at different rates, and the inability to perform as well as other children in the classroom can affect a child's self-esteem. Teachers often recite math problems orally, and each child is given a turn to answer aloud. Some children cannot solve the problem at all. Others do not solve the problem the way the teacher intended. Even though they arrive at the correct answer, their strategy may not satisfy the skill being taught, or the teacher. Children are aware of their inabilities, and it becomes quickly obvious which children are the mathematical thinkers, and which are not.

You want your child to see herself as a mathematical problem solver whether or not she is the quickest with the answer in class, and whether or not her method of arriving at the solution to a problem is the traditional one. Math phobics are made, not born. Math anxiety comes when a child is made to feel uncomfortable with numbers, and you want to make sure this doesn't happen to your child.

So what can we as parents do to help? The first thing we need to do is encourage our children to experiment with numbers. One way they can experiment at home is to count physical objects. Let them count your forks and spoons as they set the table for dinner. Let them count cans and boxes as they help you put groceries away. If all else fails, let them count M&Ms. Soon they will be ready to replace the physical objects with written numbers and to begin addition and subtraction.

Provide your child with an environment where she can freely explore a wide variety of materials and ask questions about those materials that encourage her to arrive at her own conclusions. You need not purchase anything special. Ask your child, "How many pennies are in our penny jar?" and you give her the opportunity to estimate and to count.

To help your child understand the language of math, you need to present it in a context that makes sense to her. Use her language and her experiences as a starting point to help her develop an understanding of math operations and concepts. Use her toys and household items when creating problems for the games in this section. She needs to be able to see and touch the objects she is counting.

The Department of Education's *What Works* study states, "Children in early grades learn mathematics more effectively when they use physical objects in their lessons." By using objects, your child is able to arrive at an understanding of the concept by seeing it. This is becoming increasingly important as television creates a new generation of visual learners. For math to begin making sense, children need to see that numbers actually relate to their world. With a kitchen scale and a piece of fruit, your child sees pounds. The more time spent with this type of activity, the better she will be able to understand the concepts and the application of otherwise abstract symbols.

As a parent, you can keep your child interested, even if the work is difficult, and you can help your child understand the language of math so she can succeed. Her successes will probably begin at home, but once she grows in confidence, she will carry her new skills into the classroom.

Keep your child's ability level in mind while working with her. You will not be able to force her to understand what is beyond her developmental level. You can, however, expect her to solve problems and to begin building a mathematical vocabulary through a discussion of what she has actually done.

The process of exploration is more important than the end product. The math activities in this chapter are designed to help develop creativity, imagination, and self-esteem in the process of strengthening math skills. These activities will help your child understand the facts she has memorized and those she will learn later. The games will enable her to apply these facts in the classroom and in life. Through practical investigation, your child will assess information, formulate questions, and attempt to find solutions to mathematical situations. She will be encouraged to acquire and practice her math facts in order to succeed in the activities. The games will provide your child with a positive experience using numbers and will encourage her to want to play with numbers in new and creative ways. She will develop a mathematical confidence that she will carry with her through life. Who knows, eventually, she may figure out how old Matthew's cat is. Have fun trying!

Guesstimation

Purpose: This game requires your child to visualize a completed project in order to be able to estimate how it can be done.

Materials Needed: You will need small household objects as your measurers: pencil, bottle cap, paper clip, and the like.

Number of Players: 2 to 6

Time: Allow 15 to 30 minutes.

How to Play: The object of the game is to predict, as closely as possible, the measurement of an object. Choose an item you have around the house—a pencil, a book, a bottle cap—as your measurer. One player must pick an object that is larger than the measurer, and all players estimate how many of the measurers will cover the object. For example, the player might ask, "How many bottle caps will it take to cross the television screen?" or, "How many pencils will cover the length of the bed?" Each player guesses aloud how many of the items will need to be used. Each player uses the same measurer to check his estimate, and the player whose estimate came closest to the correct number wins.

Modifications for Older Children: When playing with older children, have them develop the answer in the number of sets of an object. For example, estimate how many sets of ten paper clips will go across the kitchen table.

Hints and Variations: This game is a good place for the imagination to take over, and the crazier the task, the more fun it will be. Everyone has the same chance of winning, as no one could have any idea beforehand, for instance, how many paper clips will cover the width of the sports page of the paper. If the child has difficulty counting, one person, possibly you, could count for everyone. Your child can guess a number, and the measuring activity will give that number meaning.

Sometimes Cheryl played this game while her boys were in the bathtub. They used the soap, a face cloth, toy boats, or anything that was available to measure the bathtub.

Skills Developed: This game encourages curiosity and originality of thinking. Your child must make generalizations based on previous experiences, and he must apply what he already knows to new situations. Once he has measured an object, he will have some idea of the measurement of another object of similar size. He will use his hunches and will need to take risks and guesses. All are important in getting the most out of a math curriculum. A child who is afraid to try a problem for fear of getting it wrong will have a harder time learning math, because he will not allow himself to experiment. This game will also show him that there is more than one way to measure objects, because measurement is not used in the traditional sense in this case. He will not be using standard measuring tools such as rulers, yardsticks, or tape measures. Who knows, this game could lead to a career in engineering!

Weight a Minute

Purpose: While playing this game, your child will practice estimating and comparing.

Materials Needed: You will need a kitchen scale or a bathroom scale. The other materials depend on what is available.

Number of Players: 2 to 4

Time: Allow 10 to 20 minutes.

How to Play: The object of the game is to guess the weight of an item. Use whatever is available in your house—apples, a squash, a hammer, nails, paintbrushes. Each player guesses the weight of an object and tells the others what she has guessed. No two players may choose the same weight. The item is then weighed. If it is small, weigh it on the kitchen scale. For larger items—iron skillets, paint cans, a step stool—have your child weigh herself on the bathroom scale, record her weight, and then weigh herself holding the item. (You can make your own decision about whether you want to get on the scale yourself.) Subtract her weight from her weight plus the item, and you will have the item's weight. Calculate the difference between each estimated weight and the actual weight. The player who comes closest to the actual weight is the winner.

Modifications for Older Children: Older children might be able to do any math involved themselves, and the process will give them practice in subtraction.

Hints and Variations: This is a good way to give your child your attention while you are cooking dinner or working on a project around the house. Keep the scale handy, and bring it out whenever you want your child to "help" in your activity. If more than two players are playing, you will want to record the guesses to avoid arguments later. When playing with younger children, you will need to do the math computations.

Skills Developed: This game will give your child a better understanding of the concept of weight because she will be able to experiment by weighing many new items and by comparing them with items she is familiar with. With repeated play, Weight a Minute encourages her to estimate the weight of an object based on previous experiences with this game and helps her test the validity of her predictions. The game provides a better understanding of greater than and less than—concepts emphasized throughout school in math and science classes and on standardized tests.

Count to Twenty

Purpose: This game provides practice in counting and encourages strategic thinking and planning.

Materials Needed: You will need a game board, markers, and a die.

Number of Players: Best with 2

Time: Allow 20 to 30 minutes.

How to Play: The object of the game is to count by alternating with another player and to be the player to arrive at the number 20. The players take turns counting, with the first player beginning with the number 1. Each player may add one or two (but no more than two) numbers with each of his turns. For example, the first player says 1, the next says 2; the next says 3, 4; the next says 5; the next says 6, 7; and so on until they reach the number 20. The player who says 20 gets to roll the die and move along the game board. If your child wants to be the player to reach the goal number, he must use strategy and think ahead to the next turn in order to succeed. The winner is the first player to move all the way around the board.

Modifications for Older Children: With older children and lots of time, count to 50. If you use a higher number as the target number, allow up to five numbers to be used at a time for each turn.

Hints and Variations: Any number can be the target number, depending on the time you have available and the ages of the players. With very young children, make 10 the limit.

This game can also be played without the game board, and it is a good waiting or car activity. When you play without a board, the player to say 20 is the winner. If time allows, play again.

To make the game go faster while using the board, use two dice instead of one. Try playing it a different way each time you play. Change the target number from even to odd, or allow variations in how many numbers may be added during the round. It sounds easy, but winning takes strategy and planning.

Skills Developed: Counting is an important part of your child's math program, and it is always a good idea to practice what he is learning. With this game, your child will count by ones or twos with a goal in mind. He must be mindful of everyone else's turn and pay close attention to the numbers being used. This is a fast and fun way for him to learn how to use an old skill in a more challenging way.

I 've Got a Problem

Purpose: This game encourages your child to pay careful attention to detail, increases her attention span, and motivates her to use her creativity and imagination.

Materials Needed: No materials are needed, but you need to play in an area where there is plenty of activity.

Number of Players: 3 or more

Time: Allow 10 to 20 minutes.

How to Play: The object of the game is to create and solve word problems based on what is going on around you. This game is somewhat similar to Ask Me a Question in Chapter 3. Here, however, each player is expected both to create a math problem using what is around her and to present it in words to the other players to be solved. Here is an example based on simple observation: "One waitress is carrying two dishes. Another waitress is carrying three dishes. How many dishes are there altogether?" A more complex problem might be this: "Five cars are stopped at the toll booth in front of us. When two get through the booth, how many cars must pay before our turn?"

All players except the presenter will try to solve the problem, and the one who solves the problem first is the winner and presents the next problem.

Modifications for Older Children: Because older children have more sophistocated language, they can develop more complex problems, for example, "Six jackets were left on the playground. When one family took three of them home, the number of jackets was reduced by what fraction?" Also, encourage them to use more than one process in their problems.

Hints and Variations: This is a good game to play at the dinner table or while waiting at a restaurant. Penny liked to play with her children while they watched sports on television. It added an educational component to a leisure activity.

Since your child will not always be able to touch the items used to make the problem, allow her to use any materials around her as counters—forks, pencils, napkins—if she needs help in arriving at the answer. Since the skill of making the problem is as important as arriving at the correct answer, be sure to praise your child for her creativity.

Skills Developed: Your child will have an easier time in school if she learns to pay attention to detail. There are learning experiences all around us; you want to encourage your child to investigate, experiment, and test what she sees. This is all part of math. If she begins to wonder and develop questions about what she sees, you have opened her eyes to endless possibilities for further exploration. She will also have a better understanding of how to solve her math word problems in school once she has created them herself.

ipe Out

Purpose: This game gives your child practice with number facts while encouraging decision making.

Materials Needed: This game requires two dice.

Number of Players: 2 to 4

Time: Allow 15 to 20 minutes.

How to Play: The object of this game is to add the values of the rolls in an attempt to come closest to the number 50 without going over and without rolling "snake eyes" (two 1s). Each player, in turn, rolls the dice as many times as he wants, adding the value of each roll to his last total. He may stop at any number before 50 and name that as his total or try to roll until the totals add up to 50. The player to come closest to 50 without going over is the winner. Any player rolling snake eyes is wiped out and eliminated from that round of play.

Modifications for Older Children: With older children, you could raise the goal number to 100 or higher. If you want to encourage the use of multiplication facts, have your child multiply the numbers on the dice by each other before adding that number to the total. You can even start at 50 or 100 and have the players subtract the number on the two dice until they get to 0.

Hints and Variations: The ways of combining numbers in this game are open to any creative suggestion your child might have. Encourage him to use his imagination.

Skills Developed: This game encourages your child to develop a plan of action and to take mathematical risks. It is a fast-moving and entertaining way for your child to practice combining numbers. Making the wrong decision can eliminate him from the game, but he will see that one wrong decision does not take away from the fun of the game or the skill he has gained. Sportsmanship plays a big part in this game, and it is a good time for you to emphasize the importance of cooperation and a respect for the rights of others.

Uncovered

Purpose: This is another game to help your child practice number facts while using strategy.

Materials Needed: You will need large photographs of single objects cut from magazines (animals work well) and twelve squares of cardboard with a math question written on the back of each. The cardboard squares should be large enough to cover each photo when placed side by side over the photo.

Number of Players: 2 children and a parent

Time: Allow 10 to 15 minutes.

How to Play: You select a picture from a magazine and cover it completely with the twelve squares—three rows of four squares usually works pretty well. The squares should be blank on the side that shows, so the math problems are on the underneath side. The first child selects a square, lifts it from the picture, and tries to solve the math problem. When he removes the square, he sees a portion of the picture underneath. If he can answer the question, he may guess what he thinks the picture is. If he can't identify the picture, he still removes that square from the picture, and the next player has a turn. If he cannot answer the math question, he must put the square back into place. The second child selects a square. If he answers the question correctly, he guesses what he thinks the picture is. Play continues until one of the children can identify the object.

As the children get more and more questions correct, more and more of the picture is uncovered, making guessing easier. There may be a particular section that would help reveal an important portion of the picture, so your child must use strategy in deciding whether to choose a square from that location.

Modifications for Older Children: This game is good for all ages, but the math questions should be appropriate for the ages of the children. As this game requires a certain level of mathematical skill, it is probably best if children of the same age play together.

Hints and Variations: Vary this game to help reinforce concepts your child is working on in school. If he is working on addition, make the questions addition questions. If he is working on multiplication, make them multiplication questions. Older children may need to work with decimals or fractions.

Skills Developed: It is important that basic math facts become automatic so that your child can use them when solving more complex problems or word problems. Drill alone is not much fun, but when drill is incorporated into a game, it can be appealing. This game incorporates math facts with a puzzle in order to provide an alternative to flash cards.

High Roller

Purpose: In this game, your child will practice number facts and develop a stronger understanding of the concepts of greater than and less than.

Materials Needed: This game requires three dice.

Number of Players: 2 to 4

Time: Allow 15 to 30 minutes.

How to Play: The object of this game is to create a number that is greater than those of the other players. Each player, in turn, rolls the three dice. She then sets the die with the highest value aside and rolls the remaining two again. The higher-valued die is again set aside and the single remaining die is rolled. For example, if the original three dice show 3, 5, 2, she sets aside the 5 and rolls the 3 and 2 again. The new values on the two dice might be 4 and 1. She sets aside the 4 and rolls the 1 again. That die might show a 2 in the final roll. The three numbers to be combined are 5, 4, 2. These are combined, either through addition for younger children or through multiplication for older children, to get: $5 + 4 + 2 = 11$, or $5 \times 4 \times 2 = 40$. The player with the most points wins.

Modifications for Older Children: Older children who are learning multiplication facts can be required to multiply the first two numbers and add the third, or add the first two numbers and multiply by the third, or simply use multiplication with all three numbers. (If it has been a long time since you did this type of math, you might want to use a calculator to make sure she is correct.)

Hints and Variations: This game can be as varied as the abilities of the players. You can even try to be the one with the smallest number by using subtraction and division. Try to play a different way each time you play.

With a child who is just beginning to work with numbers, this game provides practice with the concepts of greater than and less than, as she must always determine which value is greater.

Skills Developed: This game encourages your child to look at a situation involving a combination of three numbers and to use those numbers to solve a problem. Your child will develop an understanding of the values of numbers in order to select the largest. She will analyze what she sees and execute a plan to reach a goal.

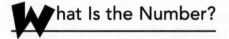

What Is the Number?

Purpose: This game encourages your child to discover creative ways to calculate numbers.

Materials Needed: You will need a game board and markers.

Number of Players: 2 to 4

Time: Allow 20 to 30 minutes.

How to Play: The object of the game is to figure out a secret number from clues given as to its value. One player chooses a number, which he keeps secret from the other players. He gives the other players mathematical clues to the value of the number. For example, if the secret number is 16, the clue might be "This number is 4 less than 10 plus 10." The older the child, the more complex the clues should be. Cheryl's granddaughter is in the first grade. When she plays this game, she uses much simpler clues, such as "This number is 2 plus 2" for the secret number 4.

Players advance 1 space on the game board for each correct answer. If the player cannot figure out the number from the clue and the clue is correct, the presenting player moves 1 space and then provides another clue. The first player around the board wins.

Modifications for Older Children: Older children might begin to use larger numbers with multiplication and division clues—for example, "This number is 16 multiplied by 301 and divided by 2." (This is another game where you might want to use a calculator to check the answers.)

Hints and Variations: The numbers used must be tailored to the ages of the players. Younger players will use lower numbers, and clues should involve addition and subtraction operations. Allow the use of calculators if you feel it is appropriate for younger players when playing against older players. This can allow the number combinations to be more complex. Include bonus (move ahead 2 spaces) and penalty (move back 1 space) squares to add an element of chance and to create more of a challenge.

Skills Developed: This game provides practice in using number facts in different ways and encourages your child to consider many ways to combine numbers. He must find new ways to present a problem when it is his turn to give clues, and when answering, he must be able to apply what he has learned.

In school, your child is frequently presented with math problems to be solved, and he will better understand them if he has practice in creating the problems himself. When he sees how problems are developed, he will be better able to rearrange difficult problems in his mind in order to change them into something he can solve. This activity also encourages a high degree of originality.

Food for Thought

Purpose: This game encourages your child to look closely at numbers and to gain a better understanding of nutritional information.
Materials Needed: For this game, use packaged food items with nutritional labels.
Number of Players: 2 to 6
Time: Allow 20 to 30 minutes.
How to Play: The object of the game is to create and solve problems from information found on boxes or cans of packaged foods in your home. Each player chooses a box or a can and uses the numbers on it to create a math problem: "If one serving of peanut butter contains 32 grams, and 9 of these grams are protein, and 5 are carbohydrates, how many grams are left for the other nutrients?"

One player writes a problem on a piece of paper and presents it to the other players to solve. The problems can be solved on paper or aloud. The presenting player does not necessarily have to know the answer herself, and answers can be checked by calculator or by you as moderator. The player who solves the problem first gets a point. After every player has presented a problem, the player with the most points wins.

Modifications for Older Children: Again, older children should be encouraged to have more complex challenges when looking at the information on the products. Encourage the use of the skills they are currently learning in school. If your child is working with fractions or percentages, encourage her to include those processes in her problems. This works best when the children are learning the same skills in school.

Hints and Variations: You might want to give points for the creation of a problem, as that is really the most important part of the game. Play at the breakfast table with a cereal box: "If there are 3 grams of sugar and 2 grams of fiber in the cereal, how much more sugar than fiber is there?" Or you can play while preparing dinner: "If you are serving macaroni and cheese and the box states that the ingredients contain 190 calories before the butter and milk are added and 290 calories with the butter and milk, how many calories are in the butter and milk?"

When you play at the spur of the moment, don't try to write the problems down. Each person can take a turn giving a problem aloud, and the other person can try to solve it as quickly as possible.

Cheryl's boys tried to get her to buy their favorite junk foods by arguing that there were so many ingredients and additives that they must be good! There are endless possibilities for problems in this game!

Skills Developed: In this game your child will use addition, subtraction, multiplication, or division to help her learn more about the foods she eats. It is never too early to educate your child about nutrition, and by playing this game, she will be practicing math facts (as well as her reading skills) while she is learning more about food values.

Combos

Purpose: This game provides practice with number facts while reinforcing skills in data collecting, organizing, and recording.

Materials Needed: For this game, you need lined paper, pencils, and two dice.

Number of Players: 2 to 4

Time: Allow 15 to 30 minutes.

How to Play: The object of the game is to roll the dice to create all number totals between 2 and 12. Each player numbers the lines on his paper from 2 to 12 down one side of the page. He gets one roll of the dice each turn and combines the number values of the dice to determine a total value. For example, if the values on the dice are 2 and 3, the player marks an X next to the 5 on the paper. The next player then rolls and records his combination on his paper. Each number on the paper must be marked as the combinations are rolled. If the combined values on the dice are the same as ones that have already been marked, the player loses that turn. For example, if a player has only the number 8 remaining unmarked on his paper, the player cannot use dice with the values of 1 and 4. Play continues until one player marks all his numbers.

Modifications for Older Children: Allow your older child to be as creative as possible in combining the values of the numbers. Dice with a 1 and 4 can be recorded as a 5 by addition, a 4 by multiplication, or a 3 by subtraction.

Hints and Variations: To increase the difficulty of this game, require that the numbers be rolled in the numerical order in which they appear on the paper, or that each number must be rolled two or three times. Younger children can be encouraged to use bottle caps or other counters to help them add the numbers if they are at the beginning stages of learning to add.

Skills Developed: This game encourages logical and sequential thinking. Each player must fill in all spaces on a score card by rolling the dice to obtain those numbers. He must also keep the final goal in mind while he progresses toward that goal. There may be many turns where your child is unable to score any points at all, and here you can help him learn the value of being a good sport and maintaining a sense of humor. This game shows many different ways to arrive at the same point, so exploration and originality are important.

Fifty

Purpose: In this game, your child practices combining numbers with a strategy in mind.

Materials Needed: To play, you will need a deck of cards (face cards removed) and a calculator (optional).

Number of Players: 2 to 4

Time: Allow 10 minutes for each round.

How to Play: The object of the game is to put down the last card that can be played without going over a total of 50 points. One player shuffles the cards and places them in a pile, face down, in the middle of the players. The first player takes two cards from the pile, chooses one, and places it face up in the center of the table. She does not show the other card to the other players. The next player also takes two cards, places one on top of the first card face up, and announces the total value of the numbers on the cards in the pile. Each player continues to draw two cards and uses them with the remaining cards in her hand. She chooses one, placing it on the exposed pile and adding the value of her card, until someone reaches 50 exactly or cannot play without going over 50. The winner is the last to play a card without going over 50.

Modifications for Older Children: When playing with older children, consider using more than one deck and raising the final number above 50. This game can also be played by beginning with the number 50 and subtracting cards until you arrive at 0.

Hints and Variations: Allow players to use a calculator if necessary to make the game go faster, and allow younger children to use bottle caps or other small items as counters. You can add an additional creative element by using the face cards and deciding ahead of time what they will stand for. For example, king = lose one turn; queen = extra turn; jack of spades = instant winner.

Skills Developed: This game will help your child feel more comfortable with numbers and will reinforce her memory of math facts. It will also motivate your child to develop strategies and to take risks with numbers, something many children are afraid to do in school for fear of being wrong.

Each move in this game involves a choice. Your child must carefully observe the cards being played and the strategy of the other players in order to determine which card to use during her turn. The skills developed in Fifty can also be applied when learning chess or bridge. Chess and bridge require players to analyze the other players' moves before deciding on a plan of attack or defense.

C olumn Counter

Purpose: This game encourages an appreciation of the concept of larger and smaller numbers.

Materials Needed: To play, you will need paper, pencils, and two dice.

Number of Players: 2 to 4

Time: Allow 10 to 30 minutes for each round.

How to Play: The object of the game is to create a number with a value greater than the numbers of the other players. Each player folds a sheet of paper lengthwise into several columns. For younger players, fold the paper into two or three columns. Third-graders might be able to work with four or five columns. At the top of the page, label the columns. Each column represents a number place value. Label the column on the right Ones, the next column to the left Tens, then Hundreds, then Thousands, and so on.

Each player, in turn, rolls the dice and records the total rolled in any one of the empty columns he chooses. Use only numbers 1 through 9; if the total is higher than 9, roll again.

The goal is to have the greatest numbers in the columns with the highest values. Once a number is placed in a column, it can't be moved. For example, if you roll a 6, you have no way of knowing whether you will roll higher or lower numbers in future turns, but you must decide where to place the 6. If you decide to place it in the column with the highest value, you must record your next number (even if it is 8 or 9) in a column of lower value. The rolls continue until all columns are filled for everyone. The player who creates a number with the highest value wins.

A sample column counter might look like this:

Thousands	Hundreds	Tens	Ones

In a sample game, if the first number rolled is 6, your child must decide where to place it. Since the lowest number he could roll is 2 and the largest is 9, 6 is about in the middle. He might place it in the hundreds column:

Thousands	Hundreds	Tens	Ones
	6		

If he rolls 9 on his next turn, he is lucky. Your child knows that is the highest possible number, so he places it in the thousands column:

Thousands	Hundreds	Tens	Ones
9	6		

On his next roll, he rolls an 8. Too bad he didn't roll that before he placed the 6 in the hundreds column. He will probably want to place the 8 in the tens column:

Thousands	Hundreds	Tens	Ones
9	6	8	

Your child's final roll is a 3:

Thousands	Hundreds	Tens	Ones
9	6	8	3

His total is 9,683.

Modifications for Older Children: For older children, increase the number of columns to correspond to the numbers they are using in their math class at school. If they are working with numbers in the hundreds of thousands, you would use six columns:

Hundred Thousands	Ten Thousands	Thousands	Hundreds	Tens	Ones

Hints and Variations: With younger children, you can use bottle caps or small toys in the columns so the child will have a better understanding of the quantity of the numbers and will be able to visualize which number is larger or smaller. Place value is a difficult concept, so don't be discouraged if your young child does not fully grasp it.

If you choose to use rolls of 10 through 12, they can be recorded as follows: 10 = 0, 11 = roll again, and 12 = player's choice. To add more variety to the game, allow your child to make up rules for 10 through 12.

As children grow comfortable with this game, they enjoy making more and more columns. It isn't long before they understand the value of 1 million.

Skills Developed: Your child needs to practice with the concept of place value in order to work with numbers greater than 9. He needs to know that although 11 is written with two 1s, it is still greater than 9. He will be creating numbers and will develop a better understanding of the values the numbers represent. The game also requires him to make decisions in placing a number in a particular location on a chart, and he must accept the consequences of his decisions, even if they do not work in his favor. He will need to make predictions about the numbers that will appear on the dice and will be able to immediately test the validity of his predictions. This game could show him the futility of gambling and save him a lot of money in the future!

Food Shopping

Purpose: This game gives your child practice with number facts and problem solving while encouraging her to become an educated consumer.

Materials Needed: You will need grocery ads from local newspapers plus paper and pencils.

Number of Players: 2 to 4

Time: Allow 15 to 30 minutes.

How to Play: The object of the game is to develop the best list of foods for the family to buy at the lowest prices. You set the budget for the game, because you want to buy the items chosen by the winner. Using the supermarket ads, have each player prepare a standard grocery list for one day's meals. This list must represent a balance of food agreed upon ahead of time—meats, vegetables, carbohydrates, and such—according to the tastes of your family members. Use ads from one or more markets, according to how you usually shop. The winner is the one who creates the best list, according to family consensus, at the lowest overall price. The prize for winning should be that the list will be used when shopping.

Modifications for Older Children: For older children, you might want to calculate price per ounce in order to discover which store or which brand or size offers the best price. For example, if a 12-ounce can of beans is $.89, and a 16-ounce can of beans is $.99, which is a better buy?

Hints and Variations: With younger children, use the numbers as they appear in the ads. Use a calculator if necessary. Cheryl particularly liked this game, as it was a big help in menu planning. It gave her a better idea of the foods her boys wanted to eat. It is best to play the game the day you plan to shop. For younger children, it is hard to wait too long before seeing results.

Skills Developed: It is important for your child to recognize that math has practical applications outside the classroom. With this game, she will need to compare and contrast prices listed and determine the lowest price. She will need to read number information critically and will become aware of how to combine numbers to provide more complete information. She will also need to convince you that her solution to the problem is the best one. This will provide an opportunity to "speak math." Careful here. If your child becomes a good comparison shopper, you may no longer be able to justify buying as many convenience foods!

Sleuth

Purpose: In this game, your child must think about how numbers fit into categories.

Materials Needed: This game requires a kitchen timer or a watch with a second hand.

Number of Players: 2 to 4

Time: Allow 10 to 20 minutes.

How to Play: The object of the game is to discover another player's secret number. One player thinks of a number, and the others must try to determine the number by asking yes/no questions—for example, "Is it an odd number? Is it greater than 2?" Players may guess the secret number after all have asked one question. If a player's guess is incorrect, the next player may ask one question and then guess. Play continues until someone guesses the secret number. The winner is the one who guesses the opponent's number first.

With 2 players, they take turns and time each other. One player thinks of a number and sets a timer to see how long it takes the other player to guess. Neither player may ask, "Is it 4?" (or 12 or 30 or any specific number) until he has asked at least three other questions in an attempt to guess the number. The winner is the one who guesses in the shortest time. If the time factor creates an unfair advantage for one player, just play for the fun of it without keeping score.

Modifications for Older Children: When playing with older children, use larger numbers, and encourage them to ask questions using multiplication and division. Allow them to use paper and pencil to help them come up with the questions if necessary. Sometimes it is easier to figure out the answer if you can work on paper.

Hints and Variations: When playing with younger children, tailor your questions to be challenging but not beyond their ability to answer. You can use this game as an opportunity to explain the difference between odd and even numbers and to clarify greater than and less than. Your child will use the information he has learned in school in new ways as he attempts to guess your secret number. If he is using a number line or counters in school, allow him to use them when playing the game.

Skills Developed: To ask questions in this game, your child will have to think about all the things he has learned about numbers and number patterns (odd and even, greater than and less than, counting by 2s, and the like). He will have to use that language to help him solve the problems. He will learn that numbers are logical and follow a set pattern but can fit into many categories (all even numbers are multiples of 2) and be used in many ways. Sleuth encourages flexible thinking.

The $1,000 Game

Purpose: This game gives your child practice in combining numbers in order to develop her ability and be at ease with them. It also shows how numbers relate to the real world.

Materials Needed: You will need newspaper or magazine ads or catalogs, pencils and paper, and a calculator (optional).

Number of Players: 2 to 6

Time: Allow 15 to 30 minutes.

How to Play: The object of the game is to "spend" an agreed-upon amount of money. Make it clear at the beginning that this is a "pretend" game, so your child will not expect to get the items she "buys." Since you are using pretend money, maybe you can pretend to play with the toys at the end of the game. A little playacting might be fun.

Set a maximum dollar goal that is meaningful to your child—$50 for a preschooler to $1,000 for an older child. Players purchase items from a catalog or from ads in newspapers or magazines. Each player records her purchases and keeps a running total. Players may "buy" only one of each item selected. The winner is the first to spend the amount agreed upon or the one who comes closest without going over.

Modifications for Older Children: As stated in the directions, when playing with older children, you should increase the target amount to a number that is in line with their ability level.

Hints and Variations: Toy catalogs are fun to use for this activity. You can vary this game by starting with the dollar amount and subtracting each time you "spend" money for an item. When you do it this way, the winner is the first person to reach 0 or the closest to it.

Use a calculator if necessary to make the game go faster, but be sure to record each transaction on paper to avoid mistakes. The sum of $1,000 is a lot of money to a child, and players may be surprised at how difficult it is and how long it takes to "spend" that amount.

Skills Developed: Combining numbers (adding, subtracting, multiplying, and dividing) is something your child does each school day, and her ability to work with numbers gives some order to her life. She will need to work with number combinations throughout school, and this type of practice can be done in a fun way, making the learning process easier. This game relates the numbers to real items, so the combinations are relevant to her world. The $1,000 Game helps her see why she might need to be involved with numbers even after she graduates from school. Anyone who has ever overdrawn a checking account can understand the value of this lesson.

Variations

Purpose: This game takes the mystery out of numbers and shows your child that there is more than one way to arrive at a correct answer.

Materials Needed: This game requires only paper and pencils.

Number of Players: 2 to 4

Time: Allow 20 to 30 minutes.

How to Play: The object of the game is to create a unique number combination that arrives at an agreed-upon answer. One player presents a number over 10 as the answer. All players must write combinations of numbers that are added, subtracted, multiplied, or divided together to arrive at that answer. They should try to think of as many combinations as possible. For example, if the chosen answer is 36, possible variations would include $6 + 6 + 6 + 6 + 6 + 6$, $40 - 4$, and 1×36. At the end of 3 minutes, players compare lists. The winner is the player with the most combinations giving the correct answer.

Modifications for Older Children: When playing with older children, use larger numbers, which provide opportunities for more possible combinations.

Hints and Variations: Allow players to use a calculator to verify answers if necessary. This is a good time to let your child use his toys or game pieces to play around with different combinations (5 teddy bears = 2 teddy bears + 3 teddy bears). Adjust the number you use for the answer to the age of the child. You can use his homework papers as a guide to determine the highest number he is working with at school.

Skills Developed: Math problems involve putting numbers together to arrive at a correct answer. This game requires your child to begin with the answer and to create the questions. By creating his own number problems, he will discover the secret of how problems are created, and this will help him determine which process to use in solving problems in his schoolwork.

Turn Over

Purpose: In this game your child practices combining numbers and develops decision-making skills.

Materials Needed: You will need two dice and all of the cards of any one suit from a deck of cards.

Number of Players: 2 to 4

Time: Allow 15 to 30 minutes.

How to Play: The object of the game is to turn over twelve cards in a suit (ace to queen). Remove the king, and place the remaining cards on the table, face up. The first player rolls the dice and turns over one or more cards to add up to the value of the roll of the dice. She may either turn over the corresponding card for each number on the dice, add the numbers on the dice together and turn over that number card, or add the numbers and turn over two cards that total that number. For this game, jack = 11 and queen = 12. For example, if a player rolls 3 and 3 on the dice, she may turn over the 6 card, or the 3, 2, and 1 cards, or the 5 and 1 cards.

The player continues rolling the dice and turning over the cards until she no longer has any cards that correspond to the numbers on the dice. If she rolls a 3 and 4 but has only a 3 card showing, she cannot make a play. When she can no longer play, she adds the values of the remaining upturned cards. All the cards are turned face up again for the next player. The next player takes her turn and adds the value of the cards remaining. When everyone has had a turn, the winner is the player whose remaining cards have the lowest value.

Modifications for Older Children: Encourage older children to use a variety of mathematical processes to arrive at the number they need. For example, if they roll a 3 and a 2, it counts as 5 if addition is used, as 6 if multiplication is used, or as 1 if they subtract. Allowing this flexibility gives older children the opportunity to use a variety of skills and to think about all the possible combinations.

Hints and Variations: At first, children may need help realizing that they can use different number combinations from those rolled on the dice, as explained in the "How to Play" section. You can vary the end result by counting the number of cards remaining, and the person with the fewest cards left is the winner. This variation affects the strategy used while playing. If you add the values, the goal will be to turn over the higher-value cards first. If you total the cards remaining, the goal will be to turn over as many cards as possible. Allow your child to use any manipulatives he is using at school—a number line, counters, etc.—if necessary.

With up to 4 players, each player could play with a different suit.

Skills Developed: Again, with this game, your child will see that numbers can be made by many different combinations. In this game, she will be limited by the numbers she sees on the dice. She will gain a better understanding of the relationship between different number combinations. She will learn to break down larger numbers into combinations of smaller numbers to understand their makeup. This type of activity encourages logical, sequential thinking and helps with determining how to arrive at the answer in word problems. Your child will learn how to take risks in math computation as she sees that there is often more than one right way to arrive at the correct answer. Turn Over encourages children to plan ahead and organize.

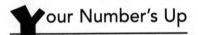our Number's Up

Purpose: This game encourages your child to discover ways to solve problems creatively.

Materials Needed: This game requires a deck of cards.

Number of Players: 2 to 4

Time: Allow 15 to 30 minutes.

How to Play: In Your Number's Up, your child uses card values in different combinations to reach a specific goal. The object of the game is to create the most problems or "books" for a given answer. All players decide on the goal answer between 11 and 14. One player deals everyone ten cards, which are kept secret from all the other players. Each card has its number value, ace = 1, and each face card = 10. The remaining cards are placed face down in a pile, with one card face up next to it. The first player draws a card. He may select the face-up card or draw from the pile. He groups into small piles (books) any two or more numbers from his hand that equal the goal answer and sets them aside. For example, if the goal is 12, the player would make books of card values that add up to 12: 2 and 10; 5 and 7; and 3, 1, and 8. Each card may be used only once. After making all combinations possible in the hand, the player must discard one card onto the face-up pile. Play continues with each player, in turn, drawing from either pile, making books, and discarding. If at any time a player runs out of cards before the cards in the face-down pile are gone, he draws three cards from that pile and begins again. When all of the cards in the face-down pile are gone, the player with the most books wins.

Modifications for Older Children: As children get older, they like to play this game with multiplication combinations, and they set a higher goal number.

Hints and Variations: Allow as many creative variations as your child might discover. Remember that the goal is to get children to think, not to win. You might award additional points for creative alternatives. The joker may be used as a wild card.

Skills Developed: Your child will be practicing his addition facts while trying to arrive at a creative solution to the problems presented in this game. He will also develop his own problems and learn to reason out problems more easily as he begins to understand the concept of addition. By choosing a different goal answer each time you play, you help your child work with and remember his number facts.

Secret Square

Purpose: This game involves practice with graphs and shows your child that graphs can be fun.

Materials Needed: You will need graph paper with large squares or paper on which you have drawn 10 × 10 grids. You will also need plain paper and pencils.

Number of Players: 2

Time: Allow 20 to 30 minutes.

How to Play: The object of the game is to locate the other player's secret square by using the points on a graph. Each player numbers the squares 1 to 10 across the top of her graph and puts letters A to J in each square going down the left side of the graph. She then marks an X or draws an object in a secret square on her own graph.

	1	2	3	4	5	6	7	8	9	10
A										
B										
C										
D										
E										
F										
G			X							
H										
I										
J										

The players, in turn, call off the letter and number that represent a particular square on the graph in an attempt to locate the other player's X. For example, a square in the middle of the graph would be at the point where the letter G and the number 4 would cross if each were extended into the graph. As each player guesses a coordinate, she blackens in that square on her own graph, so she will remember which squares she has already guessed. Play continues until one player has located the secret square of the other player. The player to locate the opponent's secret square first is the winner. This is a peacetime version of the game Battleship.

Modifications for Older Children: This game is especially fun for older children because of the strategy involved.

Hints and Variations: Although this game is designed for 2 players, younger children could pair up with older children or an adult. You might want to work in pairs with your child for the first time, so she can learn how to play from your example. The game is not as difficult as it might appear. Encourage your child to use her finger as a guide in naming the coordinates of the square. Starting at a number, move your finger down to any square you choose. Then move your finger to the letter at the side that is on that line. That number and letter are the name of the square.

Cheryl's boys enjoyed drawing objects (a soccer ball, an animal, a smiley face) instead of an X in the secret square.

Skills Developed: The ability to read charts and graphs is an important part of math classes as your child gets into middle and high school, and Secret Square will help get your child ready. This game requires her to create a graph and use the coordinates to solve a problem. Making a graph and filling it herself will help her understand information she sees in graph form. Points on a graph are named by the letters going down the side and the numbers going across the top. She has to be alert to all possible combinations of numbers and letters on the graph in order to use as many of the combinations as she needs. She has to use trial and error and experimentation to solve the problem.

rder

Purpose: This game provides practice with addition, subtraction, multiplication, and division while encouraging organizational skills and strategical planning.

Materials Needed: You will need paper, pencils, and three dice.

Number of Players: 2 to 4

Time: Allow 15 to 30 minutes.

How to Play: The object of the game is to roll all the numbers from 1 to 12 in order. This is accomplished by rolling the actual numbers or by combining any of the numbers rolled. The numbers must be rolled in order, and a 1 must be rolled before any other number can be recorded.

Each player writes 1 through 12 down the left side of his paper. Then the players, in turn, roll the three dice and check off the number or numbers they can make by adding them together. When combining numbers, players need not use all of the dice. For example, a roll of 1, 2, and 3 on the dice could be counted as 1, 2, and 3; or as 4 (3 + 1); or 5 (3 + 2); or 6 (3 + 2 + 1), depending on the number needed to complete the sequence. A player continues his turn as long as he is able to check off a number he needs. When he misses and can do nothing with his roll, the next player rolls the dice. The winner is the first player to roll all of the numbers.

Modifications for Older Children: You can increase the challenge for older players by requiring all players to go from 1 to 12 and then from 12 to 1. This is a good way to encourage the use of multiplication with older children. For example, the numbers 1, 2, and 3 could be combined this way: 1 + 2 = 3, and 3 × 3 = 9.

Hints and Variations: Allow your child to use any process—addition, subtraction, multiplication, or division—that will arrive at a desired number. The thinking that must go into arriving at the best answer is just as important as the answer, but use calculators and counters if necessary. This game is similar to Combos, described earlier in this chapter, but encourages a different way of thinking. In Order, players must roll numbers in order, and the use of three dice increases the ways the numbers can be combined. Because Order is more difficult than Combos, it might not be as appropriate for younger children.

Skills Developed: Your child has to be alert to all possible combinations of numbers that appear on the dice. He must use his roll to his best advantage, and this involves strategy. He must work in a logical and sequential manner and must determine the best mathematical process to use in a given situation.

This is the skill students need at school when working with number problems such as this one: "If Ethan is 5 feet tall and is 2 inches taller than Aaron, and Aaron is 4 inches shorter than Katie, how tall is Katie?" To solve this type of problem, your child will need to work in an organized way. Before he can begin to solve the problem, he must develop a strategy for solving it.

The Stock Market

Purpose: This game encourages your older child to practice addition, multiplication, and subtraction skills in an exciting and practical arena. The concepts involved would be too difficult for younger children, but a younger child might have fun watching.

Materials Needed: You will need the New York Stock Exchange report from the financial pages of the Sunday newspaper. You also will need paper, pencils, and file folders.

Number of Players: Any number

Time: Allow at least 30 minutes each week.

How to Play: The object of the game is to be the one to make the most "play" money in the stock market over the course of one week. The players choose a target amount of money each player is allowed to "spend." Players examine the Sunday financial page of the newspaper, using the New York Stock Exchange report to choose five different stocks. The stock name abbreviations are listed in the left-hand columns.

If players decide they will spend $10,000 each, each player must then decide how much money she will spend on each of the five stocks. One player might decide to spend $2,000 each for Coca-Cola, IBM, AT&T, Gillette, and CBS.

She must then find the price for each of her stocks in the right-hand column of the exchange report. Round up fractions of ½ and more, and round down those below ½. For example, if Coca-Cola is listed at 51¾ per share, round the cost up to $52. This player can divide her $2,000 investment in Coca-Cola by $52 to discover she can purchase 38 whole shares. Players must purchase whole shares only.

At $34 per share, she can buy 58 shares of AT&T. If IBM costs $131 per share, she can buy 15 shares. At $73 per share, she can buy 27 shares of Gillette. She can buy 11 shares of CBS at $179 per share. Because you cannot buy fractions of shares, the total "spent" will not be exactly $10,000.

After each player has selected her stocks and has decided how many shares of each she will "buy," she places her calculations and selections in a file folder.

The following Sunday, the players look up the current price of their stocks and multiply that amount by the number of shares they own of each. Next, each player adds together the value of her total stock holdings to see if she has more or less money than when she started.

The player who makes the most money wins.

Hints and Variations: If you save the stock pages over two Sundays, you can play the game in one evening by checking both day's reports. This game provides a good opportunity to encourage your child to read the business pages of the newspaper and to become involved in what is happening in particular industries in order to decide which stocks she will purchase when playing.

For those who are unfamiliar with the abbreviations listed in the daily reports, *The Standard and Poor's Stock Guide*, available in local libraries, includes the abbreviations for each company, the price range over a 15-year period, and the primary business of each company.

Even though they were not spending real money, young people we played with enjoyed this game so much that they could not wait a full week to find out how their stocks were doing. They checked their holdings each day.

Skills Developed: This game encourages your child to practice math skills in a fun way. She will see that math can relate to many aspects of her life and that the ability to manipulate numbers can be very important after she graduates. Everyone needs to balance a checkbook, some of us buy stocks or bonds, and everyone shops for groceries and tries to live within a budget.

She will be risking "play" money based on information she has learned in school or from the news on television or in the newspapers. She will become more alert to world events and how they can affect the economy.

Weather Forecasting

Purpose: This game, designed specifically for older children, helps them see how math is related to the real world.

Materials Needed: You will need the weather charts from the newspaper. Save them over a period of a week. You will also need paper and pencils.

Number of Players: 2 or more

Time: Allow 15 to 20 minutes.

How to Play: The object of the game is to choose the city with the highest average temperature over the course of one week. Each player looks at the temperature ranges on Monday's temperature chart and selects a city. Each player must choose a different city. By examining the chart for several days, he can get an idea of which cities usually have high temperatures. You can also use this as an opportunity to look at a map of the United States and discuss which cities might be hotter due to their locations.

Once the players have selected their cities, they record the high temperature for their city each day of the week. At the end of the week, they add the daily temperatures together and then divide by 7 to get an average temperature for the week. Players compare totals, and the player who selected the city with the highest average temperature wins.

For example, player 1 chooses Albuquerque, player 2 selects Dallas, and player 3 chooses New Orleans. The daily temperatures for Albuquerque are 70, 69, 71, 68, 75, 73, 70; the average temperature for the week in Albuquerque would be 71. Remainders of 5 and over should be rounded up to the next degree; averages with remainders under 5 should be rounded down. The players for Dallas and New Orleans perform the same calculations, and all players compare results to see which city has the highest average temperature for the week.

Hints and Variations: The information on the weather charts can be used in many ways, so allow your child to come up with different games using the same information. For example, you can each predict which city will have the highest, or lowest, or greatest change in temperature on a particular day. You can use the numbers of the temperature chart to make up problems and have other players solve the problems. Don't limit yourself, and use a calculator if necessary.

This game also gives your child some understanding of geographical differences.

Skills Developed: Math is more than just putting numbers together. It involves looking for patterns in information and making predictions based on that information. By using actual weather charts for these problems, your child will be able to test his predictions of real weather trends and patterns, and he will have a better idea of how math can apply to many aspects of his life.

Applying math involves taking risks and making assumptions based on information you already have. This game allows for immediate feedback regarding predictions and helps your child formulate information in preparation for future guesses.

What?

Helping Your Child Develop Memory Strategies

hat is your best friend's phone number? When is your mother-in-law's birthday? What did the neighborhood you grew up in look like? Can you name the Great Lakes? When you answer these questions, you are using memory strategies you have learned over the years. Perhaps the repetition of dialing your friend's phone number has helped you memorize it. Maybe you keep a list of important birthdays written on your calendar. When you think about your old neighborhood, you probably create a picture of it in your mind. If your teacher taught you to use the acronym HOMES to remember the names of the Great Lakes, you use a mnemonic device. All these strategies help you remember.

The development of strong memory strategies will help your child, too. Whether they help him remember the name of a playmate in nursery school or the names of the presidents, these skills are essential. Unfortunately, though almost everything your child will learn in school is related to memory, little time is spent developing memory strategies.

What can we do to help? We can expose our children to strategies that strengthen their memories. We can demonstrate how repetition will help them memorize information and how categorizing information might be more helpful. Sometimes it is easier to remember when the information is divided into manageable "chunks." Often, writing down information or drawing pictures of the information can assist memory. When children can visualize what they are trying to remember, recall is even more accurate.

The games in this chapter are designed to strengthen your child's memory skills. They give children practice in many of the strategies that will help them remember important information. Memory skills help children learn to spell, build reading comprehension and knowledge of math facts, learn important dates and facts from history, and achieve higher-level thinking skills.

Repetition is an elementary strategy that even very young children can use. When young children learn to talk, they mimic your expressions and learn new words by repeating yours. Repeating spelling words can help them remember. Though repetition is limited in its usefulness, it is appropriate for some learning situations, such as practicing the multiplication tables.

Children use chunking and categorization strategies to remember longer and more complicated information. They may break the information down into manageable sections. Young children use this chunking strategy to learn the alphabet with the "Alphabet Song," which breaks the information down into smaller, more memorable parts: "ABCD EFG HIJK LMNOP . . ." Often, they remember phone numbers the same way—the first three numbers, then the last four. Older children can chunk sections of social studies assignments. Rather than trying to remember everything about India in one session, they may divide the information into sections and then attack each chunk individually—climate, holidays, government, etc. Once they have mastered each individual chunk, they can add the next until they have learned and remembered all the information.

When children learn to categorize information, they not only improve their memory, but also begin to make abstract associations that enhance their thinking skills. At an early level, this type of strategy helps children separate numbers from letters. Later, it will help children separate information, such as animals that live in the water and animals that live on land. At a more advanced level, this strategy helps children see similarities and differences in order to integrate new information with information they have already stored.

The most sophisticated and most important memory strategy is visualization. Visualization helps improve memory in all areas; if a child can visualize something, he can remember it. When children visualize, they make mental pictures of what they would like to remember. Think of their visual memory as a videocassette tape or a DVD that can be replayed over and over when they need to retrieve information.

Some reading systems use visualization strategies to help children remember what they have read. These systems encourage students to visualize information as they read it or hear it and to create pictures of that information. Children then replay their visual images to solidify the pictures in their memories. Finally, they "retell" what they see in their pictures, and this three-step process helps improve listening skills, reading comprehension, and memory.

Visualization is difficult for most children. Living in a world where so much information is already provided in a visual format, modern children have difficulty creating images in their minds. Children who spend hours in front of the television or who read only illustrated books lose the ability to visualize. Pictures are so often provided for them that they simply don't know how to go about creating pictures in their minds. However, with practice, children can learn this important skill.

The games in this chapter encourage children to create their own images and to replay those images in order to remember information. In addition to these games, you might read your children books without pictures, or you might begin listening to old radio programs or audiobooks. This will give children opportunities to create strong images in their minds.

All of the memory games in this chapter encourage children to organize their thoughts. This type of organized thinking helps children at all levels of development. So unplug the TV, turn off the computer, and get ready to charge those memory cells. Before you know it, your child might be the next champion on "Jeopardy."

Mimic

Purpose: This game helps improve visual memory.
Materials Needed: No materials are required.
Number of Players: 2 to 4
Time: Allow about 5 minutes for each round.
How to Play: The object of the game is to recall and mimic a series of movements. The first player strikes a pose. Then, the next player re-creates the original pose and follows it with another movement. The following player recreates the original two movements and adds a third, and so on. For example, the first player might twist her body. The second player would twist his body and then reach into the air. The third player would twist her body, reach into the air, and then cross her arms. The combinations are endless. The last player who can remember and mimic all the movements wins. Play rotates.

Modifications for Older Children: This game is appropriate for all ages, as young children and older children can have fun at the same time. Giggles are sure to develop while you are playing this game.

Hints and Variations: This is a good game for young children, as playing it does not involve reading, writing, or language. It may be played both indoors and outdoors. Players could make their movements very small while playing in the back seat of a car. They could even limit their movements to their fingers or their hands. In an outdoor setting, movements can be much larger.

Skills Developed: This game will help your child focus her attention on a visual image in order to hold that image in her mind. As she mimics the pattern of movements, she uses the strategy of motor movement to improve her visual memory. Perhaps you have used a string tied around a finger to help you remember to do something. This act of tying the string helped you remember what to do.

Children can use visual sequential memory skills to remember spelling words, lists of facts, dates in history, a series of directions, etc. Outside the classroom, experience with this type of visual memory game can help a child on the athletic field. Children need a strong visual memory to recall plays and to adjust their positions in response to changes in the game.

Clapper

Purpose: This game enhances the ability to recall specific sound patterns.

Materials Needed: No materials are needed.

Number of Players: 2 or more

Time: Play usually lasts 10 minutes or less.

How to Play: One player claps his hands in a specific pattern—for example, clapping "shave and a haircut, two bits," a football cheer, or the pattern of a recognizable television or radio commercial. The other player or players take turns repeating the pattern exactly. When each has had a turn, the next player creates a new pattern, and play begins again. There are no winners or losers. Just have fun.

Modifications for Older Children: Older children might use more complicated patterns than younger children, so it would be difficult for them to play this together. Save this as a one-on-one game.

Hints and Variations: As the players become more experienced with this game, they will be able to create their own rhythmic patterns. Older players will be able to come up with complex variations. This can be difficult, as the player must remember what she created. Don't be afraid to stamp your feet as well.

Children who enjoy this game might like to learn more about Morse code.

Skills Developed: This game gives your child practice in listening and following directions. Both the player who comes up with the clapping patterns and the player who repeats them must remember the sequence. Children need sequential memory in order to follow directions, recall a series of events, remember their math facts and spelling words, and many other activities that take place in the school environment.

Although this game is based on a sound pattern, players are watching the clapper's hands. This shows that it is easier to remember things when you hear them and see them at the same time.

The Shell Game

Purpose: The purpose of this game is to help your child revisualize something he has already seen.

Materials Needed: You will need shells of various shapes and sizes and a blindfold.

Number of Players: At least 2 children and 1 parent

Time: Allow 10 minutes.

How to Play: In this game, parents act as supervisors, rather than participants. The parent presents a selection of shells—some scallop shaped, some snail shaped, some crab shells, some whelks, and so on. Have the children spend 2 minutes studying the shells. Allow the children to touch them or draw pictures of them, if that helps. Blindfold the first player. Have him sort the shells according to shape while blindfolded. Each player takes a turn sorting the shells. Children love the idea of doing things blindfolded, and this game helps them visualize and remember.

Most often, this game has no winners or losers. It is just fun to play.

Modifications for Older Children: For older children, use items that are more similar in type, so the children can be alert to subtle differences. When the items are most similar, the game is the most difficult. For example, ziti pasta and rigatoni pasta are much the same, and they will be more difficult for players to discriminate when blindfolded.

Hints and Variations: If you do not live in an area where shells are readily available, play this game with buttons, beads, rocks, or pasta. When using other items, sort by size or texture.

Skills Developed: The ability to produce a mental image of something he has seen helps your child remember. This is particularly helpful when children are trying to remember information presented in a visual format—videos, slides, DVDs, and so forth. This type of memory strategy is also useful when children are trying to learn spelling words or math facts. Once children are old enough to take notes, this type of memory skill can actually help them visualize and remember their notes.

The Shell Game also helps children notice differences. This type of visual discrimination assists them when they are trying to learn shapes, letters, or numbers. Children with strong visual discrimination skills have little trouble seeing the difference between an octopus and a squid, an African elephant and an Asian elephant, or an octagon and a hexagon, for example.

The Last Word

Purpose: This game helps children retrieve information by grouping words into categories.

Materials Needed: No materials are needed for this game.

Number of Players: 2 or more

Time: Allow 1 to 2 minutes for each round.

How to Play: The first player chooses a category and names any item that fits into that category. For example, a player might choose to name a fruit. Each player in turn must think of another word that fits the category. Play continues around until no one can think of another word that fits. The winner is the player who comes up with the last word. At the beginning of each round, a new player selects the category—for example, transportation, colors, or animals.

Modifications for Older Children: Older children can come up with more sophistocated categories. This will stretch their imaginations. They can also be required to name all of the words previously mentioned by other players.

Hints and Variations: Another way of playing this game is to use beginning sounds—cat, car, cantaloupe, etc. When children play this game by thinking of words that begin with the same sound, they also work on their phonemic awareness skills. This variation is similar to Beginnings in Chapter 1. The emphasis here, however, is on categorization and memory skills rather than phonemic awareness skills.

Skills Developed: With practice, your child can strengthen her ability to recall specific information quickly. Many classroom situations require children to come up with a quick answer to a question. Some children do this with little effort. Others can benefit from strategies to help them recall. The strategy developed here is categorization.

Categorization is a storage technique. When children learn to store information in their brains by categories, it is easier for them to recall and cross-reference the information when they need it. Just about everything can fit into one or more categories. Practice in categorizing improves memory because it helps children find the word they need to recall by finding it within its category.

The Gatherer

Purpose: This game also provides practice in categorizing as a way to help with memorization.

Materials Needed: You will need a tray or another flat, movable surface. You also will need assorted small objects, a timer or watch with a second hand, and paper and pencils.

Number of Players: At least 3

Time: Allow 10 minutes for each round.

How to Play: One player, the gatherer, takes a turn collecting the objects to be used in the game. As the gatherer collects objects, he tries to gather items that fit into several categories—for example, items made of plastic, items that are round, items made of wood. The gatherer places all the items on the tray and tells the players what categories are represented. The other players may look at the tray for 2 minutes. The gatherer takes the tray out of the room, and the players list all the items they can remember. The player who remembers the largest number of items wins the round. Each player takes a turn being the gatherer.

Modifications for Older Children: Older players may play with many more items and with a larger number of categories.

Hints and Variations: Younger children could play this game without writing down the objects they recall. Instead, they could take turns naming an object on the tray. The last player to name an item on the tray would win.

The number of items should vary according to the age of the players. Younger players might play with a few items, all from the same category. As the parent, you can determine the number of items necessary to play in order to keep the game at the appropriate level for your child.

Skills Developed: The ability to categorize will help your child understand language. When children can categorize, they can apply general information to a specific item. For example, when reading a story about zebras, it is helpful if the child already knows that a zebra is a mammal. That knowledge provides the child with information that may not be specifically mentioned in the plot of the story. This type of information helps children make generalizations.

The ability to categorize helps children store and retrieve information. Information placed in categories is much easier to recall than a long list of facts would be. The child who can break down a geography lesson into the categories of climate, economy, history, and customs will be able to recall much more about a country than the child who simply tries to remember facts. To play this game, one player must gather a group of objects, and the other players must remember the objects. As the gatherer fits objects into categories, his categorization skills are reinforced. As the other players recall the items, the ability to think of the objects in terms of categories will help them remember. For example, if you know that all of the objects you saw fit the category of animals, that knowledge will help you recall any objects you are having difficulty remembering.

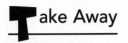ake Away

Purpose: This game works on sharpening and refining your child's memory skills.

Materials Needed: You can use whatever you have at hand if you are in a restaurant, at the dinner table, or in any other family area where there are items around.

Number of Players: 2 or more

Time: Allow 5 minutes for each turn.

How to Play: This game is ideal to play while waiting for a meal at a restaurant. Adults and children can play together. One player is chosen to begin. All the others close their eyes. The player removes one object from the table and hides it in her lap. When she says, "Ready," everyone else looks at the table and tries to discover what is missing. The first one who guesses correctly gets 1 point. That player gets to hide an item for the next round. The player with the most points is the winner.

Modifications for Older Children: This game is ideal for all ages when played on the spur of the moment. Penny enjoys playing with her children and grandchildren at family meals. When playing according to the variation in which you use items on a tray, adjust the number of items according to the age of your children. With younger players, the number might be three or four items. For older children, use five to ten items to try to sharpen and challenge their memory skills.

Hints and Variations: You can play this game at home by arranging any number of items on a tray. One player closes her eyes, and the other removes one of the objects from the tray. If the player can guess what is missing, she gets 1 point. If she cannot guess what is missing, the other player gets 1 point. Players take turns. Vary the number of objects on the table or tray according to your child's age. You might need to play a few times in order to determine a number that will be challenging but not frustrating.

Another way to play is to place the items on the table or tray in a row when showing them to the other player. The viewing player closes her eyes, and the other player rearranges the items. Then the viewing player opens her eyes and tries to put the game pieces back in the original order.

Skills Developed: Like the Shell Game, described earlier in this chapter, this game encourages your child to revisualize what she has seen to remember it. When we have difficulty remembering something, we often try to visualize where we saw it last. If we can think of where we saw it or what it was next to, we can often come up with the name of the item. There are many strategies to trigger memory, and it is important for your child to learn to use a variety of them, so they will be available to her when she needs to remember something.

Tripper

Purpose: This is another game to enhance memory and visualization skills.

Materials Needed: No materials are required for this game.

Number of Players: 2 or more

Time: Allow 5 to 10 minutes.

How to Play: You have probably played some version of this game yourself, without even thinking about the memory activity involved. The first person names a destination and an item that begin with the letter *a*. For example, the player might say, "I'm going to Alabama, and I'm going to take an apple." The next player repeats the sentence but substitutes a new destination and adds a second object, both of which start with the next letter in the alphabet: "I'm going to Boston, and I'm going to take an apple and a bookbag." The next player's destination and the third object begin with the third letter in the alphabet: "I'm going to Calcutta, and I'm going to take an apple, a bookbag, and a calculator." The more outrageous the destinations and the items, the more fun the game. Players are eliminated when they are unable to remember where they are going or what they are going to take. Play continues until only one player (the winner) is left or until you get to the letter *z*. If play continues all the way through the alphabet, all the players win.

Modifications for Older Children: This game is designed to increase memory abilities. Challenge older children to make it all the way through the alphabet.

Hints and Variations: With younger players, you could use an alphabet strip to help them remember the letters. If the alphabet is too long for them, choose one of the player's names for the game. For example, for Muffy, you could say, "I'm going to Maryland, and I'm going to take a minibike," and, "I'm going to Utah, and I'm going to take a minibike and a ukulele." Older players will use more sophisticated destinations and objects.

Skills Developed: This game provides practice in using order as a strategy to help players remember. It also fosters creativity and humor. As the child travels through the alphabet, she learns to remember information in a specific order—in this case, alphabetically. This enhances sequential memory. This game also reinforces alphabetic awareness, discussed in Chapter 1.

This type of activity helps your child learn to use mnemonic devices to help her remember. Think back to when you used the mnemonic device HOMES to remember the names of the Great Lakes (Huron, Ontario, Michigan, Erie, Superior). Giving your child the opportunity to practice this type of memory strategy will help her when she needs to remember specific information. Some children use these strategies naturally. Children who have never thought to use this type of strategy can be taught to do so.

napshot

Purpose: This game helps develop and improve visual memory and provides practice in recreating visual images.

Materials Needed: To play, you will need photographs or pictures from magazines. You will also need paper; pens, pencils, or crayons; and a watch with a second hand or a timer.

Number of Players: At least 3 (the more, the merrier)

Time: Allow 5 to 10 minutes for each round.

How to Play: The object of the game is to remember as many individual items as possible from the presented picture. One player chooses a photograph or picture from a magazine that includes many related or unrelated items. For example, a picture of a farm might be appropriate for young players. Older players might try to remember a picture of a sporting event. The player who chooses the picture acts as timekeeper. All other players study the picture for one minute. At the end of the minute, the timekeeper puts the picture away, and the players each try to draw a picture of as many of the items as they can remember in two minutes (any close approximation of the item should be accepted). The player who remembers the most items from the picture wins.

Modifications for Older Children: If older children and younger children are playing together, the older children should have less time to look at the picture.

Hints and Variations: If the children are intimidated by drawing and are old enough to write, they can list the items they remember.

If you select this option, reduce the amount of time they have to recall the picture.

If children are having difficulty remembering more than several items each time, help them to develop memory strategies. They might start by remembering everything of the same color, then everything that is soft, everything that is hard, or anything that belongs in any particular category. This categorization skill will help them with other memory tasks.

Skills Developed: This game encourages players to develop visual awareness and helps them develop strategies to improve memory. It may also help them focus on details. To play, your child must first hold a total picture in his mind. Then he will focus on the individual items within the photograph or picture in order to make a drawing of each of the items.

When children have strong visualization skills, they can use visual images to help them remember classroom presentations as well as information provided in videos or DVDs. Once they have recorded those images, either with notes or with pictures, their memory of the subject is stronger.

Commando

Purpose: This game provides practice in remembering a series of verbal directions.

Materials Needed: To play, you will need a pencil and paper.

Number of Players: At least 3

Time: This game moves very quickly.

How to Play: One player (the Commando) writes a series of activities to be completed—for example, touch your nose, hop on your right foot, wink your left eye, and then turn in a circle. That player reads the directions to the other players. The directions cannot be repeated. The other players try to act out the sequence of activities in the correct order. Each player who performs all of the activities in the correct order receives 1 point. Play rotates, and each player has a turn to be the Commando. The winner is the player with the most points at the end of the allotted time. Ties are encouraged.

Modifications for Older Children: Older players might choose to perform up to 10 actions. Older players might make their series of activities include finding a passage in a book, reading it aloud, and then acting it out. Encourage them to use their imaginations.

Hints and Variations: The activities can be simple or complex, depending on the age of the players Younger players might be able to remember only two or three simple activities. When parents play, the list might include take out the trash, put a new liner in the trash can, empty the dishwasher, and hang up your coat. However, with these activities, parents won't be invited to play too often.

Skills Developed: All school-age children need to be able to follow directions. When children have difficulty with schoolwork, it is often because they did not follow directions. This game provides practice in listening to a series of commands, visualizing the sequence of the actions required, and executing the tasks. Children will realize that following directions in school is not really that difficult and can even be fun.

Famous Folks

Purpose: This game helps children remember visual details and, in the process, introduces them to world leaders.

Materials Needed: You will need photos of people from newspapers or magazines (you can even use family photos), masking tape, scissors, and a pen.

Number of Players: 3 or more

Time: Allow 10 to 15 minutes to play, plus additional preparation time.

How to Play: You will need some preparation to play this game. Someone must take the time to collect the photos and label them. One player collects photos of important world leaders from newspapers or magazines and identifies each person by writing his or her name on the back of the photograph. If there is print on the back of the photograph, simply place a piece of masking tape on the back of the photo, and write the name on the tape. This preparation is a perfect rainy-day activity.

To begin the game, the person who has collected the photos spreads them out in front of the other players and identifies the individuals in the pictures. The person doing this says each name only once and then scrambles the pictures. Each player, in turn, selects a photo, identifies the person, confirms the answer by reading the name aloud from the back of the card, and then places the photo in his pile. If the player's guess is incorrect, he reads the correct name and returns the photo to the game. Play continues until no photos are left or everyone is stumped. The player with the most pictures wins. It is fun to play several rounds of this game using the same photos, so the players have an opportunity to remember all of the individuals in the photographs.

Modifications for Older Children: When playing with older children, use more photographs and less-recognizable world leaders. This game will also help with their awareness of current events and history.

Hints and Variations: Use the age and experience of your children to determine how many photos to use. When playing with younger children, introduce them to just a few new faces each time. You could start with the president of the United States, the vice president, and the attorney general. Each time you play the game, keep some of the individuals they recognize, and add some new leaders. The game may also be played with sports heroes or the characters from a favorite television program. This game is supposed to be fun, so be sure to include pictures of some people your children can immediately identify.

You can also use this game to help children remember relatives they don't often see. Photos of Uncle John, Aunt Jarah, and cousins Amy and Ben can be used to help refresh your child's memory before going to a family reunion. If necessary, you can give the children tricks to help them remember—for example, Bow Tie Ben or Jeweled Jarah.

Skills Developed: Children today are exposed to thousands of images over the course of a week. These images are flashed on the television screen for seconds at a time, leaving children no time to appreciate differences and details. This game enhances visual discrimination skills. Children must learn to discriminate in order to recognize countries on a map, a particular species of animal or plant, individual people, and even characters in a picture book. As children practice these discrimination skills, they improve their ability to remember visual details.

Chucky's Challenge

Purpose: This game helps children develop categorization skills while improving visual memory.

Materials Needed: You will need index cards, scissors, glue, drawing materials, and/or pictures from magazines.

Number of Players: 2 to 4

Time: Allow 15 minutes or more.

How to Play: The commercial game of Concentration is an excellent choice for improving visual memory skills, but this game takes it a step further. As with the commercial game, players must remember where a particular card is located. But in Chucky's Challenge, children try to make category matches instead of exact matches, so they are challenged to think of objects that belong together.

First, you and your child create the game pieces. You may draw objects on the index cards, or you may cut pictures from magazines and glue them on the cards. As participants are drawing or gluing pictures on each card, they must remember to find another object that falls into the same category—for example, an apple and a banana, a car and a plane, a parrot and a toucan. With younger children, you may need to help them create the game pieces.

To begin the game, the players shuffle the index cards and place them face down on the floor or on a table. The first player turns over two cards. If they do not belong in the same category, the player returns each card to the same spot, face down. The next player turns over one card and decides whether the object on the card falls into the same category as one of the previous player's cards. If it does, he tries to remember the position of the first player's card in order to make a category match. If he succeeds, he removes the two cards in that category from the game and puts them in his pile. If the card he turns over does not fall into the same category as any of the previous cards, he turns over another card at random. If the objects match, he removes the cards to his pile. If they don't match, he returns them to their original positions. As play continues, more and more objects are exposed, and the players have a greater chance of making matches if they can remember where the objects are located. The player who has found the most category matches at the end of the game wins.

Modifications for Older Children: As described in the variations, older children can play this game with a greater number of cards.

Hints and Variations: You can adjust the game's level of difficulty by determining the number of cards in play. The more cards you use, the more difficult the game. With younger players, start with ten cards, and increase the number as the children become more experienced. Older players can play with up to fifty cards.

On occasion, players will select objects that could fall into more than one category. For example, four objects could be a car, a train, a plane, and a cloud. The player who created the matches intended the plane to match the cloud as an object in the sky, but the player who turned over the plane matched it to a train as a type of transportation. When this happens, if the player can justify his match, he claims the match. The ability to explain how the two objects go together is enhanced when children must come up with reasons for their matches. When this happens, the game may end with some unmatched cards.

Skills Developed: In this game, children hone their ability to categorize, which can help them even when they are learning to read. They must know the difference between numbers and letters before they can master reading skills. As they get older, the ability to group information makes studying easier.

As children are involved in creating the game pieces, they must come up with objects that fall into particular categories. The process of making the game pieces is just plain fun.

AaBbCcDdEeFfGgHhIiJjKkLlMmNnOoPpQqRrSsTtUuVvWwXxYyZz

Bibliography

Hempenstall, Kerry. "Phonemic Awareness: What Does It Mean?
A 2004 Update." EducationNews.org, educationnews.org
/phonemic_awareness_what_does_it_.htm (accessed 12
September 2004).

International Reading Association. "Phonemic Awareness and the
Teaching of Reading: A Position Statement from the Board of
Directors of the International Reading Association." Newark,
DE: International Reading Association, April 1998.

Ratey, John J. *A User's Guide to the Brain*. New York: Pantheon,
2001.

Shawitz, Sally. *Overcoming Dyslexia: A New and Complete Science-
Based Program for Reading Problems at Any Level*. New York:
Alfred A. Knopf, 2003.

Stanovich, Keith E. "Romance and Reality" (Distinguished Educator Series). *Reading Teacher*, December 1993–January 1994.

U.S. Department of Education. *What Works: Research About Teaching and Learning*, 2nd ed. Washington, DC: U.S. Department of Education, 1987.